D0587184

How to Pass

HIGHER
English

Ann Bridges
Consultant Editor: Carolyn Cunningham

HODDER
GIBSON
AN HACHETTE UK COMPANY

The Publishers would like to thank the following for permission to reproduce copyright material:

Photo credits

p.12 © Ingo Bartussek – Fotolia; **p.21** © PAINTING/Alamy; **p.46** © Stockbyte/Photolibrary Group Ltd; **p.76** © Andrew Aitchison/ In Pictures/Corbis; **p.127** © Mander and Mitchenson/University of Bristol/ArenaPAL; **p.148** © Stockbyte/Getty Images; **p.154** © MarkaBond/Fotolia.com; **p.159** © Warner Br/Everett/REX.

Although every effort has been made to ensure that website addresses are correct at time of going to press, Hodder Gibson cannot be held responsible for the content of any website mentioned in this book. It is sometimes possible to find a relocated web page by typing in the address of the home page for a website in the URL window of your browser.

Hachette UK's policy is to use papers that are natural, renewable and recyclable products and made from wood grown in sustainable forests. The logging and manufacturing processes are expected to conform to the environmental regulations of the country of origin.

Orders: please contact Bookpoint Ltd, 130 Park Drive, Milton Park Abingdon, Oxon OX14 4SE. Telephone: (44) 01235 827720. Fax: (44) 01235 400454. Lines are open 9.00–5.00, Monday to Saturday, with a 24-hour message answering service. Visit our website at www. hoddereducation.co.uk. Hodder Gibson can be contacted direct on: Tel: 0141 333 4650; Fax: 0141 404 8188; email: hoddergibson@ hodder.co.uk.

© Ann Bridges 2014

First published in 2014 by
Hodder Gibson, an imprint of Hodder Education,
An Hachette UK Company
211 St Vincent Street
Glasgaw G2 5QY

Impression number   5 4

Year   2018 2017

Cover photo © Maksym Yemelyanov - Fotolia
Illustrations by Barking Dog Art Design & Illustration
Typeset in 13/15 Cronos Pro (Light) by Aptara, Inc.
Printed in India
A catalogue record for this title is available from the British Library
ISBN: 978 1471 808340

Contents

Introduction

The aim of this book is, obviously, to help you to pass Higher English. That's what it says on the tin –and that is what, for the most part, it does. Where the book diverges from that aim, and it does sometimes, it is moving on to a book that might be entitled 'How to Pass Higher English Well'.

There is basic information on all aspects of the examination – from little things like semi-colons to big things like Shakespeare's plays – but there are also advanced hints and advice for those of you who want to get a really good pass.

You will also find that there is a lot of cross-referencing. What you learn about writing discursive essays, for example, is reinforced by what you learn about understanding and analysing non-fiction texts in the next part of the book. And what you learn in the Understanding, Analysis and Evaluation section helps you to answer the questions on specified Scottish texts. These skills are also needed for writing your Critical Essay. And, finally, your ability to understand, analyse and evaluate your literary texts can be applied to your own writing for the Folio – so we are back where we started. Nothing in an English course is wasted! That is why it is quite important to read **all** sections of the book – not just the ones you think apply to you. The skills in English are interdependent: the difference from task to task is merely in how you apply them.

There is a mixture of all the following methods: direct teaching; hints about possible misunderstandings and mistakes; sample questions; exercises to allow you to try out what you have just learned. There are summaries which suggest what you should have learned. But, most importantly, there are **sample answers**. You can use these to check your own attempts against what is a 'good' answer. You can cheat and look up the answer before you try to answer the question. It doesn't really matter how you use them, so long as you actually read the answers **and** the advice which follows many of them. There is probably as much 'teaching' in the commentaries on the answers as there is in the body of the book.

You may find some of the vocabulary used in this book hard; some of the questions and exercises will certainly be too hard at the beginning of your Higher year. Most of the answers provide far more than you would be expected to write, but they are meant to cover a variety of possibilities. As you know by now, there is no such thing as the one and only 'correct' answer to questions on English texts. All the components of this book provide resources for your learning and for the enhancing of your potential as an English student. But you have to do the learning. Teaching has no value unless accompanied by your active engagement.

Folio of writing

As the folio of writing is the first finished product that you have to generate as part of your external examination for Higher English, we will look at this first.

You have two essays to produce: one broadly 'discursive' and the other broadly 'creative'. Each is marked out of 15. You have a considerable amount of time to prepare and produce what will count for 30 per cent of your marks, so it is not a good idea to leave everything till the last minute.

How you work on your folio and the deadlines you have to meet will be controlled by your centre.

This part of your exam attainment is the one that is most closely within your control. It is probable that, given time and effort on your part and with appropriate support, you can write two essays of pass standard. The advice that follows is designed to help you in the process, but it goes further than that. There are tips here to help you do better. Some of the advice is quite detailed, especially towards the end of the section – but extra marks are valuable and you can gain them in your own time without being under pressure in the exam hall.

The process of your writing may be monitored in a variety of ways, and as a result of varying teaching contexts, but your topic and your draft(s) will be overseen. You should use advice given on your draft(s) and also make sure that you are acknowledging all your sources. You must avoid plagiarism. There is a document about what this means on the SQA website, so that there is no excuse for not adhering to the conditions.

The technicalities – the easier part

1   Your essay should be accurate in its use of language – punctuation, sentencing, spelling, capitalisation should all be correct. You have plenty of time to go over your work with a fine toothcomb and with a dictionary. Remember that you are allowed to use such tools as dictionaries and a spellchecker. But beware of accepting blindly what a spellcheck program suggests – sometimes it will give an alternative that is not what you meant. And it cannot distinguish between such things as the correct/incorrect use of *its/it's*, *their/there/they're*, etc.

2   Your essays should be within the specified word limit – 1,300 words. There is no excuse for presenting over the word limit. If you do go significantly over the limit, markers are told to stop reading the rest, and so you are penalising yourself. An essay without an effective ending is missing a vital component.

3   Your essays must be presented by the correct date.

> **Hints & tips** ★
> If you haven't already done so, read the Introduction at the start of this book, because it gives you useful advice on how to use this book effectively.

> **Hints & tips** ★
> The number of marks available for your Folio (30) is the same as the number of marks available for the Reading for Understanding, Analysis and Evaluation exam paper (30), which you will sit in May. So it makes sense to make a good effort in writing.

> **Remember**
> These three technical items are always within your control.

Hints & tips ★

The SQA's definition of technical accuracy for folio pieces is as follows:

Few errors **will be present: paragraphs, sentences and punctuation will be** *accurate and organised* **so that the writing can be** *clearly and readily* *understood;* **and** *spelling errors (particularly of high frequency words) should* *be infrequent.*

If your pieces do not meet the conditions for technical accuracy, the highest mark your essay can get is 8 out of 15 no matter how good the content, story, argument, etc.

If you compare this with the requirements for technical accuracy for the critical essay (page 137) you will see that the folio one is a bit more demanding. This is because you have time to redraft and think about your folio pieces, which you do not have under exam conditions when writing your critical essay.

The content – the more difficult part

Your writing at Higher level must be appropriate for purpose and audience, follow a line of thought based on relevant research/experience/ knowledge of genre and be expressed in language appropriate to convey thought/argument/emotions/concerns clearly. Add to that some of the words necessary to achieve highly in this area:

- strong degree of mature reflection
- insight
- sensitivity
- command of thematic concerns
- genre features used skilfully
- strong impact.

Your essay(s) should be informed and relevant for your audience – that involves, in some cases, the collection and organisation of your data/ material/ideas; in other cases it involves the exercise of the imagination and the capturing of feelings and emotions.

One piece of writing must be what is broadly classed as 'discursive'. This will be one of:

- an argumentative essay
- a persuasive essay
- a report for a specified purpose.

The other piece of writing must be what is broadly classed as 'creative'. This will be one of:

- a personal essay
- a reflective essay
- an imaginative piece.

Discursive essays

Argumentative essay

This kind of essay follows an 'argument' – not in the sense that you may have a row with a friend, but in the way that you have come to understand the meaning of the word in your Critical Essay work. The 'argument' of a play, or a poem is really the thought process that involves the audience/reader in increasing their understanding of the play or poem.

In an argumentative essay, therefore, the exploration of a particular topic should have as its purpose the wish to inform, expand and clarify the reader's thoughts.

The important word here is 'exploration'. When you set out to write on a topic that interests you, you will already have some ideas about it. But probably your information is fairly superficial – perhaps a chance television programme, or a family discussion, or a topic touched on in class. You need to explore the ideas further, and then to guide your reader through these ideas.

Very occasionally, you may be such an expert in your field that you do not feel the need to do any research – say you come from a family of farmers and have discussed endlessly some of the issues associated with the Common Agricultural Policy, but perhaps you (and your family's) views might just be a tiny bit biased. The same applies to those of you whose family consists of tree surgeons, teachers or taxi drivers. Generally, essays written off the top of your head may be interesting, but will lack substance.

Several topics may have been suggested to you in the course of your studies, and discussed in class, but you still need to do your own research, and present your own ideas and conclusions.

Research

This is the first tool of writers of non-fiction – biographers, essayists, historians, social commentators and newspaper reporters to name but a few. And that now includes you.

As with all research, you may find that your original ideas about your topic are wrong, or only partially proven, or too cut-and-dried. This is one of the values of research – if you have a truly open mind you may have to change it!

The research tools at the call of a modern writer are truly amazing. With a click of a mouse, or the touch of a screen, a mass of material is available. But that advantage can also be a disadvantage. If there is too much, where do you start? Your training should enable you to go to reputable sites, back catalogues of 'serious' newspapers, books (check the writers' credentials), downloads of documentaries from reliable sources (which does not include everything on YouTube).

Hints & tips

*Make a note of **every** single book, article, site, etc. you consult **as you read it**. Although you may only use a fraction of what you read, you must be able to put the references for what you do use in your bibliography.*

Research is betrayed as shallow when a bibliography records only one article from a tabloid newspaper and a reference to Wikipedia – although Wikipedia can be useful and can provide a good starting place for deeper research.

You can also use interviews and oral material, but again, you must record your sources.

Statistics

You may wish to back up your argument by the use of statistics – it is a ploy used by politicians, reporters and persuaders of all types. This is a valid use of evidence, but only if you have found the statistics in a reputable source and checked them at least once in other places.

As an example, look at this headline and subheading from October 2013:

AN ARMY OF DRUNK 11-YEAR-OLDS SWAMPING A&E DEPARTMENTS

Nearly 300 children aged 11 and under were admitted to A&E departments in the last year

On the face of it, 300 is a shocking statistic, but, is this really such a big number? There are 365 days in the year. So less than once a day, throughout the whole of the UK's hospitals, one child was admitted as 'alcohol related'. There are 700,000 11-year-olds, so the percentage of such children admitted is only 0.04 per cent. And 'alcohol related' could mean not 'drunk', but a stone-cold sober child injured by someone who was drunk.

This headline is at least based on some actual figures, but there are far less reputable organisations (and reporters and politicians) who distort numbers past any point of truthfulness. For this reason it is your job, as a researcher, to check statistics against other sources. If the whole of your argument is based on a false statistic, which you have found but not checked, your essay will carry little weight.

As you were gathering your material you may have strengthened your original point of view, or moderated it a bit because of information that does not fit with your original thesis, or you might even have 'changed sides'.

Once you have decided what your point of view is, you now want to transmit it to your reader.

Organisation

Look at your notes/headings/extracts/statistics/evidence. You have probably gathered more material than you are going to be able to use. But that can be a good thing for two reasons.

1 You will be able to select the strongest points to promote your idea and fulfil your purpose.
2 You have a confidence-boosting command of your subject, which will allow you to change, rearrange or expand a point later on.

How you make a survey of your material is entirely up to you. It depends partly on whether you are basically a 'spatial' person or a 'list' person. Some people see connections in a spider diagram, and some in lists or tables.

Whichever of these you choose, you then have to select and arrange the points in a sensible order. Some of these are described below.

In an argumentative essay you are required to take at least two viewpoints into consideration, and treat each fairly. This does not mean that your own personal preference or point of view has to be suppressed. You can be fair, but you can also be very firm in your conclusion so long as it can be justified from the evidence you have presented.

In its simplest form you can deal with some points 'for' an idea/theory/ campaign and some points 'against'. Then you reach a conclusion that gives your own point of view, arising from the evidence you have presented.

This form has the advantage of clarity, but perhaps becomes rather 'listy' – **adding** ideas together rather than **developing** them.

Exercise

Here are six negative points you might have found in your research for an essay about the pros and cons of providing children with laptops, gadgets, phones or games involving 'screen time':

1 expense
2 physical inactivity
3 lack of socialisation
4 isolation from family
5 stranger danger
6 creation of attention deficit

You could simply write a paragraph about each of these items, then follow that with a number of advantages that you have found, and thus reach a conclusion based on the strength of each 'side'. This becomes simply a matter of addition, not of development.

Alternative approaches would be to:

● start with the less important items, building up to the most important (A) ⇨

Hints & tips

*Your choice of organisation depends on your material and what it is that **you** want to say to your reader. The important thing is that you have to think about your organisation, and try out various methods until you find the most satisfactory in terms of impact, interest and clarity.*

⇨
- start with the really important, eye-catching item, then provide more evidence, again perhaps building up from the trivial to the more important ideas (B)

Try to arrange the six items above in order to achieve development A.

Then try development B.

Another possible pattern is where each paragraph or section of the essay contains opposing points on one aspect of the topic. This keeps a balance in the argument, and can make things clearer to the reader.

Linking

The linking of your ideas is, of course, an important aid to the development of your essay. There are numerous 'signpost' words that are useful both in your writing folio and in your critical essay work:

- **numeric:** *firstly, secondly, and finally*
- **contrasts:** *but, on the contrary, on the other hand, conversely*
- **intensifiers:** *and even more so, moreover, furthermore, without doubt*
- **causality:** *because of this, therefore, as a result*
- **time:** *once, in the past, nowadays, later, in the future.*

All of these are useful, but they should not be used slavishly or monotonously. You would be unlikely to use 'fifthly' or 'sixthly', for example. And there should certainly be strict rationing of 'furthermore' and 'moreover', which are often used mechanically and so become devoid of meaning or impact.

Often a more natural linkage is not dependent on single words or phrases, but in the continuation of thought from one paragraph to the next – you will come across many examples of this in your study of non-fiction texts for analysis (see pages 43–45).

For example, in an article about buying children gadgets as Christmas presents, the link is made by the repetition of the idea of 'technology':

> …*Sociologists suggest that our increasing use of* **technology** *is making us more distracted and less able to be intimate with those around us.*

> **This technologising** *of Christmas, and our lives, can be* **charted** *through the list of the most popular gifts over the years…*

Try out various links. Don't be satisfied with the first one that comes to mind. There might be a more forceful (or a more subtle) way of doing it.

Use of illustration

Presenting a familiar, human interest example to engage the reader's emotions is another familiar device. For more on this see pages 47–48.

Use of language

Generally the language of an argumentative essay should be fairly formal, both in vocabulary and sentencing. But it is acceptable to depart from normal usage in order to make a point more effectively and forcefully.

Persuasive essay

Many of the above steps are also necessary if you attempt the next suggested form of discursive essay – the persuasive essay.

This is probably best attempted if you have really strong feelings on your topic, and are convinced that your ideas are the right ones – even in the face of contrary evidence. Most teenagers perhaps would recognise this position!

Research

You still need to do some research – partly to find more evidence for your standpoint, but also to uncover any really obvious errors you might fall into. If you make a really unwarranted statement such as 'All unemployed people are benefit scroungers', you will not shock the reader into taking your views seriously. You are more likely to put her or him right off continuing to read your essay. Your evidence should be 'reliable' but it can be massaged, 'cherry-picked' or exaggerated a little to make your points.

Organisation

See the advice given on page 5 on how to deal with your research.

When you have completed the survey of your research, you then have to select and arrange your points in a sensible and effective order to achieve your purpose – **persuasion**. The successful organisation of a persuasive essay is just as varied as that of an argumentative essay – and it depends on which audience you are trying to persuade.

Three possible patterns are:
1   Stick only to the evidence that supports your view, suppressing everything else. If you do this sufficiently intensely and forcefully, your reader may be carried along by your language and not stop to think of any contrary points.
2   Provide, in the course of your essay, a few counter arguments (preferably rather weak ones) and then immediately demolish them. This can give the appearance of having taken everything into account, and therefore might make your essay more convincing.
3   Start out with seeming to accept the opposing view, lulling your reader into a (false) sense of security, before you gradually pile on the hammer blows for your own argument.

There, are, of course, many other ways of approaching your material. Again, you should experiment with different ordering, different climaxes until you find the one with most impact.

Hints & tips

Before you hand in your final version, look at the advice under 'Editing' on pages 24–26.

Linking is important in a persuasive essay, and all the suggestions on page 6 are useful. Added to those are such words as '**essentially**', '**effectively**', '**clearly**', '**basically**', '**obviously**', '**naturally**'. These words, at the beginning of a sentence, are designed to presuppose that the reader will agree with what follows. This can leave the readers with no chance to think for themselves about the point of the sentence.

Rhetorical devices

On top of these there is a special class of techniques that are especially useful in this context of persuasion. They are often called 'rhetorical devices' and include the following:

- You are probably familiar with the idea of the rhetorical question. This is used to suggest that the answer to the question is self-evident; it is the writer's answer, and the reader is expected to agree with it.
- The climaxing of items in groups of three is often used as it seems to appeal to some deep language structures that we all recognise. Here is an example from an article entitled 'Have Foodies had their Day':

  The fact remains, however, that despite the growth of farmers' markets, despite Jamie Oliver's ardent crusading, despite Michelle Obama's organic vegetable patch, gastroculture has done markedly little to improve the eating and cooking habits of most.

- The use of climax to strengthen or exaggerate an idea.
- The use of anti-climax to puncture an 'oppositional' idea.
- Repetition of all kinds, including a 'choral' start or finish to several paragraphs (as heard in Martin Luther King's 'I have a dream' speech). The danger with this is that such a device, unless used skilfully, can become mechanical and/or boring and predictable.

Use of language

It is possible to use more relaxed, informal language in a persuasive essay if it is part of a deliberate effect.

Use of illustration

Presenting a familiar, human interest example to engage the reader's emotions is another familiar device (see pages 47–48).

Use of statistics

See the advice on use of statistics in Argumentative essays (page 4).

> **Hints & tips** ⭐
>
> *A good test of the impact of your persuasive essay is to read it out loud to someone else, or even to yourself in the mirror. Are you convinced? If you are not, it is likely that others won't be either.*

Report

This form of writing, more perhaps than the previous two kinds, depends on how exactly the purpose of the report is matched to the expected reader. At Higher level, success is more likely if the purpose and audience are carefully defined, remembering always that the writing has to demonstrate the ability to encompass complexity and detail. There should be clear conclusions drawn from detailed evidence, taking into account, where necessary, possible alternatives. The language in which the report is written is likely to be used with exactitude, but is less likely to demonstrate a wide spectrum of language devices. Extra material in the form of statistics, graphs, etc., well explained and integrated, can add to the success of the piece.

Creative essays
Personal essay

On the face of it, this may seem an easier option than writing an imaginative piece. After all, you don't have to dream up ideas – you know who is involved and you know the story because it is about you. It is about your own experience.

One of the problems with personal writing is that there are two purposes that are easily confused:

- **Writing as therapy**, where an attempt to record an experience is good for the emotional health of the writer.
- **Writing as art**, where the recording of an experience creates interest, sympathy, surprise and understanding in the reader (remember, the general heading for this type of essay is 'creative').

Occasionally, the first type (therapy) does meet the criteria for 'art'. It has to say something of more than merely personal significance. That is, it has to say something important to readers which has the potential to expand their understanding of some aspect of 'life, the universe and everything'.

But too often the therapy type of writing simply describes a sad event in the person's life, told in great detail, with an added-on reflective paragraph about the lessons learned from the experience. This kind of essay will usually struggle to pass.

Here's an example of this kind of tacked-on ending:

> *I get upset every time I think about him not being there. One thing he taught me is never to take life for granted because you never know how long you have. If it wasn't for my grandad fighting his battle against illness and putting a smile on his face every day, I wouldn't be the person I am today. He taught me that no matter how bad things seem, enjoy life while you have it.*

This does not mean that writing as therapy is of no value. It is one of the gifts that literacy gives us. We can attempt to come to terms with the agony and the ecstasy of our own lives through writing accounts, poetry and song, and it is good for us. But it may not be good creative writing. It is good enough for us, but not for a wider audience. So perhaps such a piece is not the best you can do for your folio.

Writing a personal essay that is 'creative' demands some of the elements of shaping and structuring that you would use in a short story. As in a short story, you do need to 'characterise' the other people in your

> **Hints & tips** ★
>
> *The personal essay at Higher level should show a degree of reflection and a sense of the writer's personality.*

narrative. You also have to be careful about considering the words you choose, and the impact of description, imagery and, possibly, dialogue.

Many submissions are related to death or divorce. These are difficult situations, and cause profound feelings of loss and despair, but to transmit those feelings effectively to a reader is quite difficult.

Suppose you have been writing about the death of your grandmother, and at some point you say 'I miss her so much'. How is that 'missing' felt? In the emptiness of a room? In a message that never comes? In a missing place at the table? These are details that make much clearer, and more poignant, the actual 'missingness' and may cause the reader to empathise with your experience.

Another common topic is an event from early childhood. The event has remained in the memory, but the element of hindsight and distance takes the edge off the sharpness of the experience. A 6-year-old does not think or see things in the same way a 16-year-old thinks she or he saw them.

Suppose that, in the course of such an essay, you remember (aged 6):

> *My father started to cry. I had never seen him cry before. It was heartbreaking.*

The third of these sentences does not ring true. As a 6-year-old, these would not have been your words. You might have been confused, scared or curious but you would not have said (or thought) 'It was heartbreaking'. Your memory, or your language, or both, are not carrying a feeling of authenticity to your reader. She or he is left unmoved.

Remember

There is a whole list of common phrases which, while true, are not particular and individualised enough to convey to an outsider (your reader) a feeling of empathy or sympathy — they become a little like a cliché. Here are a few such phrases:

- ☞ *He was my best friend ever.*
- ☞ *I was being torn in two.*
- ☞ *She was always there for me.*
- ☞ *He always understood.*

Hints & tips

Before you hand in your final version, look at the advice under 'Editing' on pages 24–26.

There can, however, be very powerful writing in this genre in the hands of a writer who is willing to work, shape and craft the experience – sad or happy – into a piece of 'creative' writing.

Reflective essay

A reflective essay is based on your experience of a particular topic, idea or thought as it has been demonstrated in your own life. The important distinction between this kind of essay and a discursive essay is that the topic has had a part to play in your own life. It could be:

- a reflection dealt with in a concerned or contemplative tone – an insight into the nature of an aspect of society adding to your understanding and self-knowledge arising from your own experience

or

- a reflection on aspects of life and your place within it dealt with ironically, whimsically or humorously, such as:
  - an essay on possessions/fashion and how important they are to your self-image
  - an essay on the trauma caused by separation from your life support system – your mobile phone.

There is a possibility that this kind of essay can veer into the discursive, but the element of personal experience keeps it firmly within the reflective zone.

Example 1

Here is the opening of an essay entitled 'Am I a Patriot?'

> My grandfather was a patriot: all his generation, it seems, were and are. He was fluent in several languages and loved to travel – but although he never belittled other countries, his was the greatest nation on earth. It was the place he felt at home, the only place that really did everything right.
>
> My grandmother, too, on the other side – she was a patriot. She would mutter under her breath about 'that Gobbles and Hitler'. Woe to anyone who, playing with model battleships, let the Bismarck win. She travelled too – though never to Germany – but she always yearned for home. Her own house, the talk of her own people, these were the things that mattered.
>
> Both, I am sure, wanted me to love my country – their country.
>
> But my grandfather was English through and through. He admired the Empire – believed that the British were somehow better at many things than those over whom they once ruled. My grandmother regarded herself as one of those people who my grandfather's race had ruled – or oppressed – for she was, through and through, a Scot, from the island of Lewis.

The body of the essay goes on to look at the different characteristics of the English and the Scots as illustrated through his own experience and comes to a conclusion:

> I do not resent the English. I cannot – I loved my grandfather, and much of my blood is their blood. But can I love them? Individually, of course – they are people like any others. But as

a nation, I cannot. I might respect them for their achievements but they are the people who viewed my ancestors, on my grandmother's side, merely as remote highlanders.

But I cannot love Scotland either. My grandmother and her people are hidebound, narrow and limited. Their concerns are often petty – and their moaning is never-ending.

. . .

I have seen the homes of my ancestors from both sides of the barriers. I cannot hate what I have seen, but I cannot choose a side because I have seen both sides through the eyes of the other. I can never reject those places my grandparents loved. If I accept one fully, I would have to reject the other, and this is impossible for me. So, in the end, I answer the initial question of the title of this essay. I cannot choose and so I cannot be a patriot.

Because the viewpoint throughout is based firmly in the writer's own and his family's experience and emotions, this is a reflective essay with strong discursive elements. It should cause the reader to have a second thought about her or his own views of patriotism, and so it is effective in achieving its purpose.

It also demonstrates the qualities of characterisation (you can 'see' his grandfather and grandmother) and has structural strengths in the way the end recalls the beginning and the title.

This kind of reflective essay would be acceptable if you are thinking of putting together a Creative Writing Folio as part of the Advanced Higher English course next year.

Example 2
You could imagine a similar essay dealing with your relationship with your smartphone.

Opening:

> *I will not be like other people. I will never own a smartphone.*
> *I will . . . what did you say? It does **that**? Let me see!*
>
> *Handed over.*
>
> *Hooked.*

In very short order this sets the scene for the discussion, and you already have a feeling for the personality of the writer.

followed by:

. . . (the case **for** smartphones – in personal terms)

> *But . . .*

followed by:

. . . (the case **against** smartphones – in personal terms)

Conclusion:

> *Purring by my side, glowing in the dark – my best friend.*

As a reader you know which side has won, and something about the self-knowledge (or lack of it) of the writer. It has said something interesting to readers (the potential audience), which has the purpose of making them look at the topic with a fresh insight.

> **Hints & tips**
>
> Before you hand in your final version, look at the advice under 'Editing' on pages 24–26.

Imaginative piece

This essay can be in any genre you have practised and feel comfortable with. The most common forms are considered in the next section.

Short story

This is one of the genres of imaginative writing that you have probably been writing since you were in primary school. Looking at this genre as practised by professional writers can help to inform your own writing.

The techniques of prose fiction are covered in Chapter 5 in the section on Critical Essays (page 143). The most important devices to consider are **plot**, **structure**, **characterisation** and **setting**. Ideally, you should be able to look at your own work in the same way that you have looked at the work of professional writers.

Plot

The hardest aspect of short stories is plotting. There are often many good and promising openings, lots of subtle characterisation, atmospheric settings, great tension or suspense. But quite often this all leads to a predictable, banal or impossible ending – a suicidal dive off the high building, which is roughly equivalent to the primary school ending: 'I woke up and it was all a dream!'

Here is an example of this kind of artificially 'surprising' ending to a short story called 'The Scream'

I passed through the chipped and peeling gates to my new school. A newspaper blew into my side. I read the headline. It read 'RIP to Jade Wilson who died age 15 on the 13th of March 2003'. That's me, I thought, but then what made it worse was the date of the paper, 13th of March 2003. My name is Jade Wilson. I died ten years ago.

Effective plots have to do more than carry the story – they should allow the theme(s) of the short story to emerge. How will the reader's understanding of the human condition be enlarged by your story? Will your reader's sympathies be engaged by your character(s) and their fate(s)? Will reading leave your reader content/shocked/amused/sad/apprehensive?

Suppose, for example, that you have decided to write in the science fiction genre. Perhaps the plot concerns some cataclysmic event threatening the human race caused by our misuse of the environment. Is your writing powerful enough to create sympathy for the protagonist(s), or to generate anger directed at the 'misusers'?

Remember

There should be nothing in your story that does not contribute to the final purpose of the story. Anything that you mention, as part of the setting or details of the incident, should be there for a reason. If you note on the mantelpiece of the room a large brass ornament, that ornament has to be used, or deliberately not used. It cannot – in a classic narrative structure – be ignored once it has been mentioned.

Methods of narration

There are various methods of narration that you can use. The most common are:

1 first-person narrator
2 third-person narrator – omniscient or restricted
3 a split narrative
4 a framed narrative
5 a reliable or unreliable narrator.

These methods are illustrated using the following scenario.

A large man enters an office to start a new job. His boss is a woman who has employed him for reasons that perhaps are not clear. Pressure of some kind has been put on her. His experience in the employment causes some form of mental breakdown.

Methods 1 and 2 are quite straightforward. Methods 3, 4 and 5 are a bit more complex and need careful handling.

Method 1

First-person narrative appears to be an easy option, as you can let the reader know the inmost thoughts of your main character. But it has limitations.

- It can become monotonous – I did, I felt, I saw.
- It is more difficult to paint a clear idea of the thoughts of others (although dialogue may help).
- It does not allow for action at which the 'I' is not present.

Using our office scenario:

I walked into the room for only the second time. The interview had been different. This was the real thing. A mixture of anticipation, anxiety and curiosity filled my thoughts as I walked towards my new boss, hand held out in greeting. She ignored it, scanned me from top to toe, frowned and left the room.

The story may then go on to catalogue the trials and tribulations of the protagonist in his first day in a new job, but because it is a first-person narrative, we don't have any means of knowing what the boss actually thinks. There are ways round that:

- dialogue where the boss says what the problem is
- an incident from which the reader can infer the boss's thoughts
- a device, such as note left on a table or an email on a screen.

but you have to be aware that there are problems to solve.

Method 2

Third-person narrative is the most common narrative method for fiction. An omniscient narrator can tell you what everyone is thinking and provide a straightforward reading.

> *He walked into the room for only the second time. The interview had been different. This was the real thing. A mixture of anticipation, anxiety and curiosity filled his thoughts as he walked towards his new boss, hand held out in greeting. She ignored it, scanned him from top to toe, frowned and left the room, asking herself if she had done the right thing in hiring such an untidy, shambolic specimen. She had been leant on heavily to give him the job but perhaps she should have resisted the pressure.*

Here, you can see both sides of the incident, but perhaps the omniscient narrator has let us see too much, too soon.

Method 3

A **split narrative** can help to achieve a compromise between first- and third-person narratives, but it is quite difficult to handle and can hold up the pace of the narrative.

> *I walked into the room for only the second time. The interview had been different. This was the real thing. A mixture of anticipation, anxiety and curiosity filled my thoughts as I walked towards my new boss, hand held out in greeting. She ignored it, scanned me from top to toe, frowned and left the room.*
>
> *What can I have been thinking of? He looked mildly untidy at the interview, but this – he doesn't even look clean. It's one thing to do a favour for an old friend's son – OK, more than a favour, a necessary recompense, a gun to my head – but . . .*

The problem is how you sustain a narrative like this without it becoming too bitty, and eventually monotonous. The key, of course, is to keep the momentum of the story going, not just cutting it up arbitrarily into chunks. You can use contrast, parallels or reversals to develop your two narrators, who have to carry a convincing narrative/plot line.

Method 4

A **framed narrative**, or a narrative using a framing device, can also be effective. It allows you to make the reader look more objectively, perhaps, at the main character. It often reveals the fate of the character right at the beginning of the story, so that you focus on the process of how he got there.

In this example, the speaker in the framing device is a psychiatrist who is treating the main character in our office scenario after his breakdown.

> *My first sight of him was when he slid silently into my consulting room as if on a breath of insubstantial wind. Over the next weeks and months I never did have a solid grip on his ethereal presence or on his equally ethereal mind. His story slipped and changed shape as we talked, but I had the impression of some*

Hints & tips

A restricted third-person narrative is one where all the events in the book are seen from the point of view of the main character. An example of this kind of writing is Ernest Hemingway's For Whom the Bell Tolls in which the main character Robert Jordan carries almost all of the actions and thoughts in the novel. The restricted third-person narrative has the same difficulties as a first-person narrative — you can only know what he or she knows/sees/hears personally.

utter truth – hidden from both of us. When I pieced it together much later it began to make a kind of crazy sense. What follows is as near as I can get to a coherent pattern and chronology.

What follows might be the story of the big shambolic guy and how through some strange conflict with his employer he has been stripped of his physique, personality, sanity even – and perhaps what form his terrible retribution took, leading to the 'consultations'. The end paragraph returns to the psychiatrist.

As I say, I tended to believe him, in the face of all the evidence. In the twists of his labyrinthine mind, he was right, and he was justified. His very quietude convinced me personally. But to my everlasting shame, in my professional capacity, I had to throw him to the wolves. And I did.

Method 5

A **reliable or unreliable narrator** – the general assumption is that the narrator – first, third, split or framer – is going to be reliable. If the narrator is going to prove to be unreliable, the writer should give the reader some hint to follow, and even if the revelation of the unreliability comes at the end it must be credible. It is not a 'Get out of jail free' card.

Structure

A sound structure can help your plotting to achieve an effective shape.

Hints & tips

Paragraphing is just as important here as it is in discursive essays. You may not have 'topic sentences' in the sense that you need them in discursive writing but each paragraph has a part to play in providing stepping stones for understanding a character, for moving the plot on or for providing a contrast important in a conflict.

Characterisation

In a short story, which usually concerns itself with one defined incident, you don't usually need a large cast of characters. As one of the basic elements of short-story narrative is conflict, you generally need at least two, but, of course, the main character can be in conflict with himself or with his environment rather than with another human being.

What she or he does, says and thinks, and what is said about or thought about her or him are the usual elements of characterisation, but not necessarily all of these, and we often don't need physical characteristics unless they are going to be important in the narrative.

> *She was blonde, about 30, with dark blue eyes.*

Probably this description is unnecessary, as it is just a standard description of an attractive young woman, whose looks may, or may not, be important for the plot.

> *A face too long, eyes too wide, too pale. First impressions are sometimes wrong – and sometimes not.*

If that description were to be used, it would be **because** there is some sort of excess suggested – perhaps a character who overdramatises or goes too far.

Setting in place/setting in time

As with the physical descriptions of characters, the first question you need to ask yourself about setting is: do we need to know? The second question is then: how much do we need to know? Consider the following:

- If your scenario is an office, it is likely that this will become obvious from the activities described, without the setting having to be described explicitly.
- If, on the other hand, your story is set in the past, or the future, your reader might find it helpful to be given that information sooner rather than later.
- If you choose to start your story with an evocative description of a place, there has to be a purpose behind it.

Example

In the following example from a short story called 'Drifting', the first paragraph, with its description of a branch and a beach, is justified by the following paragraph in which the characters appear in the setting. When you reach the end of the story, it is obvious that the first paragraph is setting up the symbolic nature of the last paragraph.

> *The ancient and smoothed branch bobs gently in the push and pull of an oncoming tide. Its surface is bleached and featureless, long since removed of all the blemishes that once identified it, and now it floats alone on a vast grey featureless plain. With no direction of its own, and no vitality in its dead core, the branch is swept towards a beach by strong currents that it no longer has the strength to fight. It moves yet more slowly now in the shallows of the small bay. It is here that it will rest, after the next high tide.*
>
> *The branch nudges lightly against a leg. The leg stands upright in the water, unflinching despite the cold. The skin on it looks*

delicate, like an old sheet of parchment, a memorial of lives long in the past; it is as much lacking in vitality as the log. Further up this leg is the hemline of a faded summer dress, the colours shadows of ancient buds. The dress hangs limp against a frame that in days gone by was full. Her face was once radiant, her lips deep, and her hair an intense copper. Now everything is grey and withered, her lips blue.

The boy standing and watching the woman from a distance is me.

The central part of the story gradually reveals the dementia of the grandmother and the effect of this on the boy who loves her and cannot bear to see her suffer.

The concentration of pain that I see all around her, the remains of humanity long past its span, drive me to crave her freedom.

I feel an overwhelming urge to give these shadows an end, to allow them to escape into nothingness.

My grandmother turns to me. In her eyes there is light but also fear. She doesn't know where she is or who I am. I smile. Bidding her follow me, I take her by the arm and lead her through the dunes and back up towards the path, and the cliff – and the edge.

Night comes with a storm. Rain beats down on the ground, washing the sand and the dunes and the cliff. The wind has changed. The water becomes rough and the log is thrown by wave after wave. The churning water grows higher, the wind faster, never subsiding. The log is cast high in the air, its end spears deep into the beach and it is buried by wave upon wave and then sand.

In the pale and pink light of dawn the still-wet sand is smooth. The log is gone. In the sand it rests protected and out of reach; no longer bothered by the cruelty of the wind or the sea. It has achieved peace.

The forms of short stories we have looked at in the last seven pages are probably those most familiar to you. There are, however, many other forms – post-modern forms, magical realism, stream of consciousness – which you can attempt if you have discussed and practised them. You can also try other forms of prose fiction – a chapter from a novel, for example – but you must always be aware of the conventions of the genre you have chosen.

Poetry

There is no reason why you shouldn't try to write in this genre. It is the most concentrated expression of ideas and emotion, but it is a craft you have to practise. Not all poems that you write will be good enough to present as an item in your folio.

Poetry versus poetic prose

The main problem is that many of the pieces of poetry typically written for the folio are, in fact, not poetry at all, but merely prose chopped up into lines to look like poetry. This arises from the idea that 'free verse' looks just like that. But if you compare a professional's use of free verse with many of the poems submitted there is a vast difference – mainly in the sound, the 'rightness' of the pauses.

Student example

Night comes with a storm.
Rain beats down on the ground
washing the sand and the dunes and the cliff.*
The wind has changed.
5 The water becomes rough
and the log is thrown by wave after wave.*
The churning water grows higher,
the wind faster, never subsiding.
The log is cast high in the air –
10 its end spears deep into the beach
and it is buried by wave upon wave and then sand.*
In the pale and pink light of dawn
the still-wet sand is smooth.
The log is gone.
15 In the sand it rests protected and out of reach;*
no longer bothered by the cruelty of the wind or the sea.*
It has achieved peace.

If you try saying the student and the following professional extracts out loud, you will realise that Ferlinghetti's lines force you into getting the sense of the movement of the eye over Klimt's painting.

The first extract you will recognise as the same words used in the end of the short story 'Drifting' on page 19. It is poetic and it has been chopped up into lines – but it is not poetry. Although full of description, it has several long lines marked with an asterisk (*) which are difficult to say, and there does not really seem to be a reason for their length.

Professional example

The Kiss – Short Story on a Painting of Gustav Klimt (extract lines 1–25)

They are kneeling upright on a flowered bed

He

    has just caught her there

      and holds her still

5 Her gown

    has slipped down

      off her shoulder

He has an urgent hunger

His dark head

10   bends to hers

    hungrily

And the woman the woman

  turns her tangerine lips from his

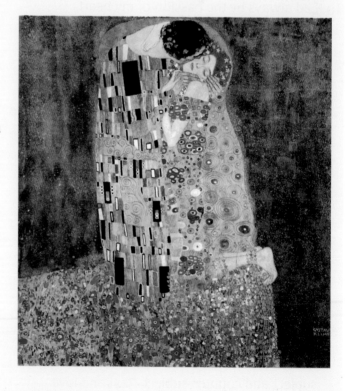

  one hand like the head of a dead swan

15 draped down over

    his heavy neck

the fingers

  strangely crimped

  tightly together

20 her other arm doubled up

  against her tight breast

  her hand a languid claw

    clutching his hand

  which would turn her mouth

25   to his

Lawrence Ferlinghetti

The other difference of course, is that the Ferlinghetti poem is describing something about a physical relationship, which, in very deft and swift lines, sketches in the characterisation of the man and the woman. The reader becomes an observer of the action. The student extract about the log is not really doing anything except giving a description. On its own it has very little to say to the reader.

Poetry in a particular form

You may choose to write in a particular form, such as a sonnet, a ballad or in rhyming couplets, but the problem in the less successful attempts is that the rhyme and form become the weights that hold the poem down with twisted phrases and unlikely words. Look at the two examples below.

Student example

Hoping always to see your eyes track me down

Through the long reaches of the coming day

I find instead my eyes on you do frown

Waiting for the response from you to come my way.

5 Why do I always have to make the first move

Your avoiding me seems to me so cruel.

What do I have to do to prove

My love for you needs no more fuel.

It will burn for you eternally in a flame

10 Fed always by the passion of my heart.

Even in the face of your indifference

My love for you will stay the same,

As right from the beginning, right from the start,

Although I know you only keep me on sufferance.

Professional example

Suburban housewife

She practises a fugue, though it can matter

to no one now if she plays it well or not.

Beside her on the floor two children chatter,

then scream and fight. She hushes them. A pot

5 boils over. As she rushes to the stove

too late, a wave of nausea overpowers

subject and counter-subject. Zest and love

drain out with soapy water as she scours

the crusted milk. Her veins ache. Once she played

⇒

⇨

10 for Rubenstein*, who yawned. The children caper

round a sprung mousetrap, where a mouse lies dead.

When the soft corpse won't move they seem afraid.

She comforts them; and wraps it in a paper

featuring: *Tasty dishes from stale bread.*

Gwen Harwood

* Rubenstein was a famous pianist and composer.

If you compare these two poems, both in sonnet form, you can see that the second, by a professional poet, is infinitely better. Not only does it flow naturally, with the rhyme acting subtly as a substructure to give form to the poem, but it is also saying to the reader something quite profound about lost hopes, the trap that closes on 'the housewife' persona. No words are wasted. The trapped mouse is important, and so is the headline featured in the last line. The reader's understanding of the housewife and her predicament is expanded by the poem.

In the first 'sonnet' you can see the forced word order to accommodate the rhyme in lines 3 and 6; the problem of trying to find a rhyme for 'indifference' in line 11; several lines that are too long to say with any ease. Overall, the poem says very little. Almost every line is a cliché, and there is no sense of a particular idea or person. Everything is generalised. The reader, in this case, has really not learned anything, so the poem has failed in any 'purpose' it might have set out to fulfil.

Remember

By all means try poetry, but beware of these two major pitfalls:
☞ Is it poetry, or is it just poetic prose?
☞ Is your attempt at form/rhyme imposing too much on the subject matter of your poem?
Read your poem out loud to help you detect problems.

Drama script

There are several forms this genre can take.

Self-contained scene/sketch

Most of the advice about short stories also applies to this form. That is, the piece of writing has to say something important to the potential audience, which has the purpose of expanding our understanding of some aspect of life or to make us look at something with new insight. Within this genre, plot, structure and characterisation have to do the same job as in a short story.

It is actually quite difficult to manage all this within the course of a dramatic script. You normally do not have a narrator. The story must unfold though the dialogue of the characters, which does not allow you to take shortcuts into letting the audience read their thoughts.

There are ways round this.
- You can have a narrator as a character.
- You can use soliloquies or asides to the audience.
- You can use stage/technical directions.

All of these, however, need to be handled with care – too many stage directions often mean that the dialogue is too weak to carry the line of thought/emotion. Soliloquies and asides do not belong to the 'naturalistic' genres on stage, so they can only be used in genres that 'allow' them. A narrator can be quite tricky to handle. She or he acts as an intermediary between actor and audience, but also distances the actors from the audience. This can prevent (sometimes deliberately) the audience's sympathies from being maintained.

Monologue

Monologue may appear to be an easier option, but, in fact, it isn't. A monologue is often just a first-person narrative delivering a not very effective story. So all the problems that arise in trying to write an effective first-person narrative in fiction also apply to monologues. The stage directions are the only technique that differentiate the monologue from the short story. While these directions can suggest events offstage, the plot, structure and characterisation still have to be skilful and creative.

Remember

Your layout of such details as speakers/stage directions/technical specifications should be clear and in line with the conventional ways of dealing with a drama script.

Hints & tips

Advice for all dramatic scripts

Speak them out loud. Get friends to read them out loud. Do the words sound as if they are the words of real people? Would anyone actually say that? This is the final test you must apply to your work. If it fails this test then you have to rewrite it.

Editing

Technical aspects

This process is almost as important as the writing was in the first place. When you have what you think is your final draft, there are several checks that you must make:
- **Capitalisation** has to be consistent. Names of places and people are easy, but names of organisations and events are more difficult. If you are writing a political essay about Parliament, the Church, the

State or the Law, you have to remain consistent. In sporting terms, the League Cup or a Grand Slam have to have their capital letters. It is just a matter of taking care. Its most important function is, of course, at the beginnings of sentences.

- **Spelling** has to be checked, either in dictionaries or by spellcheck – but remember that spellcheck can get it wrong if your initial spelling is too far from being correct. And it can't pick up on common errors such as *of/off*, *there/their*, *it's/its* which can let you down so badly.

- **Sentencing** that is poor means your writing may not communicate meaning at first reading. There are many rules to help you to get your sentencing right. If you are unsure, one helpful test is to look at each sentence you have written – from the capitalised word at the beginning to the full stop at the end. Read it out loud in isolation from the rest of your essay. Does it make sense? Where you pause to take a breath is often an indication that there should be punctuation of some kind. Is there? Should it be a comma or a full stop? The answers to these questions will create more accuracy in your writing. It will take some time to treat each one of your sentences in this way, but it will be worth it. Note that, in some essays and in some styles, sentencing may not be standard, and this is perfectly acceptable if it is effective in creating an impact.

- **Proof reading** is essential. After all your editing and care, if you leave obvious typos, they will be counted as errors. You may say that your finger just hit the wrong key, or the paste command did not do what you wanted it to do. But all that is your problem. They are your errors, not the computer's.

Remember

If your pieces do not meet the conditions of technical accuracy, the highest mark your essay can get is 8 out of 15, no matter how good the content, story, argument, etc.

Structure and organisation (especially in discursive essays)

Paragraphing is important in giving shape to your essay. For each paragraph you need to ask yourself:

- What is the topic?
- What are the points being made?
- How does the paragraph help to develop the overall argument?
- How does each paragraph link with the next in a logical way?

And for the whole essay ask yourself:

● How does the overall structure of the essay promote the conclusion?

In Chapter 3 Reading for Understanding, Analysis and Evaluation you will find a more detailed discussion on the use of topic sentences (page 34); how points are made (pages 40–42); how arguments are developed (pages 42–43) and in what ways links are effective (pages 43–46). See also the section about the effectiveness of a conclusion on pages 48–50.

Cutting out unnecessary detail

At its simplest, a personal/reflective essay that begins:

I was so looking forward to this holiday. The morning we were leaving for the airport, my brother Tommy decided he was feeling sick, but he was bundled into the car anyway by my frustrated father and my harassed mother, along with my baby sister Eveline. We just got there in time to check in and then we were able to relax with a cup of coffee.

is going to have bored the reader within three sentences. Whatever does or does not happen on the holiday has nothing to do with the journey to the airport. The whole paragraph is unnecessary and could be cut.

Advanced editing (trying to make the already good essay even better)

Style

Below is an example of how advanced editing of the essay 'Am I a Patriot?' (pages 11–12) can make a piece of work that is quite effective as it stands even better. You can see how word order and sentence structure can be altered to make the ideas have more impact.

Original ending

I have seen the homes of my ancestors from both sides of the barriers. I cannot hate what I have seen, but I cannot choose a side because I have seen both sides through the eyes of the other. I can never reject those places my grandparents loved. If I accept one fully, I would have to reject the other, and this is impossible for me. So, in the end, I answer the initial question of the title of this essay. I cannot choose and so I cannot be a patriot. (91 words)

Hints & tips

These pages are aimed at trying to get the best possible result in your creative writing. You may have written a really good essay already – but perhaps you can still do better. This process is one which you might adopt in a Creative Writing workshop, or which could be very useful if you were thinking of going on to Advanced Higher next year.

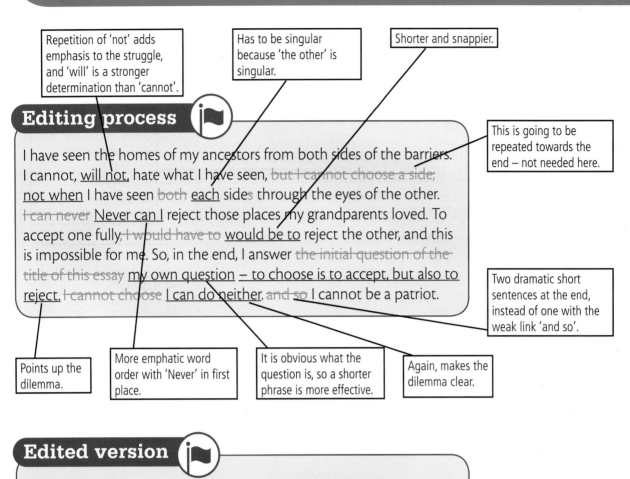

Editing process

I have seen the homes of my ancestors from both sides of the barriers. I cannot, <u>will not,</u> hate what I have seen, ~~but I cannot choose a side;~~ <u>not when</u> I have seen ~~both~~ <u>each</u> sides through the eyes of the other. ~~I can never~~ <u>Never can I</u> reject those places my grandparents loved. To accept one fully, ~~I would have to~~ <u>would be to</u> reject the other, and this is impossible for me. So, in the end, I answer ~~the initial question of the title of this essay~~ <u>my own question – to choose is to accept, but also to reject.</u> ~~I cannot choose~~ <u>I can do</u> neither. ~~and so~~ I cannot be a patriot.

Callouts:
- Repetition of 'not' adds emphasis to the struggle, and 'will' is a stronger determination than 'cannot'.
- Has to be singular because 'the other' is singular.
- Shorter and snappier.
- This is going to be repeated towards the end – not needed here.
- Two dramatic short sentences at the end, instead of one with the weak link 'and so'.
- Points up the dilemma.
- More emphatic word order with 'Never' in first place.
- It is obvious what the question is, so a shorter phrase is more effective.
- Again, makes the dilemma clear.

Edited version

I have seen the homes of my ancestors from both sides of the barriers. I cannot, will not, hate what I have seen, not when I have seen each side through the eyes of the other. Never can I reject those places my grandparents loved. To accept one fully would be to reject the other, and this is impossible for me. So, in the end, I answer my own question – to choose is to accept, but also to reject. I can do neither. I cannot be a patriot. (88 words)

Cutting out unnecessary words/phrases

For the really skilled and ambitious writer, the most important task is to cut out unnecessary words, however good they might look. Take as an example the paragraph we have looked at already on page 18 from the short story entitled 'Drifting'.

Original first paragraph

The ancient and smoothed branch bobs gently in the push and pull of an oncoming tide. Its surface is bleached and featureless, long since removed of all the blemishes that once identified it, and now it floats alone on a vast grey featureless plain. With no direction of its own, and no vitality in its dead core, the branch is swept towards a beach by strong currents that it no longer has the strength to fight. It moves yet more slowly now in the shallows of the small bay. It is here that it will rest, after the next high tide. (101 words) 'removed of' doesn't make a lot of sense, and does it matter that it once had 'blemishes'?

'vast' is not needed, as 'plain' on its own suggests a large expanse.

The tide is coming in, not out: pull is confusing.

Repetition of 'featureless'. Is this clumsy, or does the repetition reinforce the idea? The answer could be either, but the question should be asked.

Editing process

The ancient and smoothed branch bobs gently in the push ~~and pull~~ of an oncoming tide. Its surface is bleached and (featureless), ~~long since removed of all the blemishes that once identified it, and now it floats~~ floating alone on a ~~vast~~ grey (featureless) plain. With no direction of its own, and no vitality in its dead core, ~~the branch is swept towards a beach by strong currents that it no longer has the strength to fight:~~ it moves yet more slowly ~~now~~ in the shallows of the small bay. It is here that it will rest, ~~after~~ at the next high tide.

Why does the branch move from 'bobbing gently' to 'swept . . . by strong currents' then back to 'moves yet more slowly'?

'after' suggests two tides, not one.

There has been no shift in time, we are still in the present.

Edited version

The ancient and smoothed branch bobs gently in the push of an oncoming tide. Its surface is bleached and featureless, floating alone on a grey featureless plain. With no direction of its own, and no vitality in its dead core, it moves yet more slowly in the shallows of the small bay. It is here that it will rest, at the next high tide. (64 words)

This is a much better piece of writing; although the effects are still a little bit overdone, the writing is consciously attempting to use the resources of language in a detailed and complex way, and to a large extent it succeeds.

Reading skills

Not surprisingly the best preparation for approaching a reading exam is to read. But how much? How often? You have to practise reading as you have to practise any other skill.

There are, of course, questions that you have to learn how to answer, but unless you can practise reading a lot, and regularly, until you are comfortable with the kinds of texts you may be faced with, the questions will remain difficult.

The first necessary skill is to gain an **overview** of an article on a topic or an account of an event.

After that each **paragraph** will contain a step in the 'argument' of the piece.

Finally, each **sentence** will contain some detail necessary for a full understanding of the text.

Overview

You will make a more positive start on your first reading of a piece of prose if you know, before you begin, what it is about. Newspapers use headlines for this very purpose. They also use subheadings and highlighted extracts, all of which are meant to catch your eye and seduce you into reading further.

Example 1

THE TRUTH ABOUT LIFE AS A HOUSEHUSBAND
200,000 British men now stay home to look after the children

So what's it like being a man in a woman's world? **Jon Absalom,** *who gave up his career, tells all!*

These three items (the heading, subheading and introduction) all stand out typographically in the article so that before you read it, you know the subject will be about dads who stay at home, and the possible problems associated with such a lifestyle choice.

Your reading will now be an **informed** reading, giving focus to your thoughts.

Example 2

FATHERS SPURN PLAN TO SAVE PARENTS FROM COURT BATTLES

Government unveils scheme to encourage mediation in contact rows

In this case you know to expect some explanation of an attempt to get (separated) parents to agree about contact time with their children instead of going to court. You also know that some fathers don't think the plan will help them much. As a result you will be on the lookout for what the plan is and why the fathers are against it. Again, you start your reading with some knowledge of what is likely to appear. You are informed and focused.

Note: 'typographically', 'spurn' and 'mediation' are words used on page 29 and this page. If you don't know what they mean, look them up. And don't worry. The more you read, the more familiar you will become with such 'high order' words.

Training for reading

You can train yourself into being a good reader, just as you can train for a sport or a craft. It may not initially be very pleasant, but if you stick with it you will make progress.

If you already read most of a quality daily paper or most of one of the Sunday 'heavies', and a couple of novels a month, with an occasional biography or historical/scientific text thrown in, not to mention two or three Shakespeare plays by way of bedtime reading, then you probably don't need to read the next section. But if that is several miles away from describing what you do, then you should keep right on reading.

Exercise

1 Find a newspaper or magazine article that attracts you because of the headline, the subject, a photograph or some interesting graphics.
2 Look at the headline, any subheadings, highlighted quotations, photo captions, etc.
3 Ask yourself: 'What do I expect to find out by reading this?'
4 Read the article.
5 Ask yourself: 'What have I found out?'
6 Write down the main ideas in note form.
7 Consider if there are any clues about the writer's stance on the topic.

*The kind of articles you need will be found in newspapers such as the **Herald** or the **Scotsman**. Weekend editions, especially the **Sunday Herald**, contain thoughtful articles reflecting on the news stories. These are probably a better source than the original news story as there is more likely to be an 'argument' rather than simply an account of events. Other possibilities include **The Times**, the **Guardian**, the **Telegraph**, the **Independent** and their Sunday counterparts including the **Observer**. Comment and lifestyle sections often offer good opportunities. There are also periodicals which cover special interest groups such as **New Scientist, The Economist, New Statesman** and the **Spectator**. Reputable sources on the internet can also provide you with similar reading experiences.*

Depending on the difficulty of the article you have chosen you might find that you have understood most of what is said, in which case you can answer the questions and move on.

If you are having difficulty, is the lack of understanding because:

a) you don't understand some of the vocabulary?

b) you get lost in the line of thought?

If (a) is the problem, get down to it with a dictionary. If (b) is the problem, read each paragraph individually, and see what meaning you can make of it.

When you have done that, give the article a final reading and see if you can make better notes (step 6 on page 30).

Repeat this exercise weekly till the exam. Even though you don't feel you are making progress, you will be. Like training for anything, doing a little often is more effective than a big blitz just before the competition.

Another way of approaching this exercise is to give the article to someone else to read after you have read it – anyone who has reading skills equal to or better than your own – and tell them what you think the main points are (long-suffering parents, friendly adults, charitable elder sisters or brothers). You are having to put your thoughts into words, and if your 'sharer' comes up with other thoughts and ideas then the interaction will add to your understanding of the piece.

If you find yourself understanding the articles 100 per cent at first reading, you need to move on to more difficult articles or to articles on subjects you know nothing about, so that you have to work harder. As in all training – no pain, no gain.

Approach to Reading

Training Programme for Close Reading

Preparation

Note down   Headline

> [ ]

Note down   Subheadings

> [ ]

What do I expect to find out from reading this article?

> [ ]

Action   Now read the article.

Result   What have I found out? Write down the *main* ideas (in note form).

> [ ]

Evaluation   Did I find out what I expected   Yes   No

How difficult was the reading?   Hard   OK   Easy

Writer's stance

> [ ]

Summary 👍

Reading for overview of information

1 Pay attention to the headline, and any bias you detect in it.
2 Look at any subheading to see what it adds about the detail or direction of the article.
3 Check the whole article for any further phrases/extracts that have been highlighted typographically for hints about important detail.

When you go through the above procedure, it means that your first real reading of the article will be focused on the main ideas – it will be **active** reading, not **passive**.

Below are two examples for you to try.

Example 1

GLASGOW'S INDOMITABLE SPIRIT IS ITS ETERNAL STRENGTH

In many times since the war, Glasgow's mettle has been tested and our people not found wanting

Out of two centuries of inequality and heavy blows – warmth and sense of optimism still exists

❓ Question

● What do you expect to find out from reading this? (**Answer (1)** on page 36.)

Example 2

IN SEARCH OF THE TRUTH ABOUT MODERN FATHERHOOD

There are still plenty of failures out there – across every class and in every town. But most men are trying very hard to be the fathers they imagined themselves to be

'A great dad can build, a bad dad can stunt, a dreadful dad can ruin'

❓ Question

● What discussion do you expect in this article? (**Answer (2)** on page 36.)

Reading paragraphs

Paragraphing is the writer's tool for giving you 'the story' in manageable sections. A new paragraph can signal any of the following:

- the introduction of a new idea
- the contradiction of a previous paragraph
- an additional development of the topic
- an opening of a new point of view in an argument
- a conclusion.

Look at the example below from an article about househusbands.

> *Last week, a report found that there are now in the region of 200,000 househusbands in this country: I am one of them. Like blue whales, we rarely meet and when we do, we cluster. I know about eight other househusbands, although, to be pedantic about it, most of them are part-timers, splitting the domestic stuff with their partners. And part-time is not full-time; there is a profound difference. I have abandoned my career to raise our son and, perhaps one day, his sibling. When I fill in forms now, under occupation I write 'househusband'.*

The topic of this paragraph is that there are now a number of men who stay at home to look after their children.

> *It is difficult being a househusband; certainly more difficult than I had imagined. The practical aspects of parenting – naps, meals, baths, bedtimes – are well established. None of it is the least bit difficult, once you know how. But a lot of it is boring. And the hours . . . they start when it's dark and cold, and they last for an unreasonable amount of time. There is little time to yourself; no time for mulling over your emails, or surfing the web, or popping out for some pleasure shopping. There's no breakfast and a shower before work. You live and sleep on the shop floor.*

The topic of this paragraph is that being a househusband is difficult. The rest of the paragraph lists some of the challenges.

> *When I do get ground down, when it feels really relentless, I have to be reminded that this is not for ever and that I'm travelling emotionally, if not geographically. I'm learning about myself, developing the patience and sympathy that I never even thought I lacked. Best of all, Jack and I like each other. I'm always pleased to see him. We spend nearly every waking hour together, yet when I'm not with him I miss him. I know what 'poi' and 'sha' mean. Above all, I know in every bone of my body that I will never regret this. I will not lie on my deathbed and think, oh, how I wish I'd spent less time with my son.*

The topic of this paragraph is that it is not all gloom and doom. The rest of the paragraph gives the most important plus point.

These three paragraphs have informed you of three steps in the argument about househusbands.

1 There are now a lot of men who are staying at home to look after their children.
2 It is not a particularly easy task.
3 But there are some great compensations.

The advantage of being able to perform this kind of paragraph identification quickly is that it allows you to see the main items without getting bogged down in detail. It takes practice. You could add it to the exercise on page 32. Choose two or three paragraphs, try to identify the topic of each and see how they link together in the argument. Help is available in your ability to spot the obvious linking words – ones that you yourself will be familiar with from your own writing (page 6).

Hints & tips

Argument *is used here in its academic sense or literary sense – as we have already discussed on page 3. It means the structure or framework of a discussion on a topic.*

Summary 👍

1 Identify the topic of each paragraph.
2 Look at the sequence, the linking, and see how the argument develops.

Reading sentences

Sometimes you have to find your way through a particularly long and complex sentence rather in the same way as you have just learned to look at paragraphs. You have to find out the important or main idea that the sentence contains. As each paragraph has a topic sentence, so a sentence has a **subject**. The subject is the thing or person the sentence is going to tell you about.

Here is a typical long sentence:

Feeling that they have failed to be the fathers they hoped – and becoming mildly depressed because of this – modern dads are increasingly avoiding emotional involvement with their children: one quarter said they never talked about personal issues with their child at all.

What is the subject here, and what are we being told about it?

The first thing you can do to simplify the sentence is to ignore the part between the two dashes – the part in parenthesis. Then you can take out the part after the colon as it is an expansion or example of what is dealt with in the part of the sentence preceding it.

So the sentence becomes:

Feeling that they have failed to be the fathers they hoped, modern dads are increasingly avoiding emotional involvement with their children:

Who is the 'they' referred to in the first few words of the sentence? It has to be 'modern dads', so the **subject** of the sentence is 'modern dads' and we are told that they are avoiding emotional involvement. The important idea therefore is that modern fathers avoid emotional involvement.

The rest of the sentence after the colon gives an example of this (not talking to their children) and the bit in parenthesis, between the two dashes, tells us that the situation has a bad effect on the fathers (they become mildly depressed).

Summary 👍

1 Try to identify the main 'subject' of the sentence.
2 Look at what you are being told about the subject.
3 To simplify the sentence you can temporarily ignore parts in parenthesis, or examples, lists or explanations.

Answers

Answer (1) (page 33)
The article will look at Glasgow people's response to adversity, despite the difficulties (possibly economic) it faces.

Answer (2) (page 33)
The article will deal with the aspects of fatherhood where the outlook is optimistic, but it will also look at the effect of 'bad' parenting.

Hints & tips ★

If you become an expert reader and master the skills we have been looking at in this chapter, you will be much more able to find your way through an article on your own, with little (or no) support from questioning on the article. This is the situation you will have to cope with when reading the second passage in the Reading for Understanding, Analysis and Evaluation exam paper.

Reading for Understanding, Analysis and Evaluation

The work in the previous chapter should enable you to grasp the general subject and argument of a piece of non-fiction prose – an article, or an extract from a longer work. In the actual exam paper you have to sit, however, you are required to show that you can understand the **detail** and the **effectiveness** of the writing you are presented with.

Hints & tips ⭐

If you haven't already done so, read the Introduction to this book, because it gives you useful advice on how to use this book effectively.

Exam paper

You will be presented with two pieces of writing that deal with the same topic or theme. There will be questions on one of the passages, and a question (or questions) that ask you to compare the two passages in some way.

There are 30 marks awarded to this exercise, and you have 1 hour 30 minutes to complete it.

The three skills of 'understanding', 'analysis' and 'evaluation' are dependent on each other, and it is perhaps a little artificial to separate them out. For example, in the following paragraph from an article about modern approaches to childhood, the question about it has two parts but the overall answer involves demonstrating all three skills.

> *And yet our panic about childhood betrays a deep ambivalence, too. Our children are in danger, fattened on fast food, corrupted by commerce, traumatised by testing. And, at the same time, other children are dangerous, malevolent beneath hooded tops, chaotic in the classroom, perilous on the pavements. Before we can have a sensible debate on child-rearing, we need to unpick which of our anxieties truly reflects the reality of the situation.*

(?) Question

- Explain what are the two views of childhood stated here, and analyse how these two views are effectively brought to our attention.

The first part of the question is concerned with your **understanding** of the main opposing ideas in the paragraph; the rest is asking you to **evaluate** the success of the writing by **analysing** aspect(s) of the language. Thinking about both parts of the question can help you towards demonstrating that you have fully understood the paragraph.

Analysis

The fact that you have two parallel sentences, one with 'our children are in danger' and the other with 'other children are dangerous', shows that there is a **contrast** between two views of children.

The **lists** which follow these statements give us a vivid picture of the number of things adults fear. The **alliteration** in each of the phrases that make up the lists add to the fear. Take the phrase 'traumatised by testing'. Without the alliteration 'testing' could be seen as a fairly neutral word, but linked by sound to 'traumatised' it makes the experience sound quite terrifying.

Understanding

As a result of your analysis you are helped towards your **understanding** of the paragraph, i.e. the gap between these two views has to be taken into account so that what really is worrying about the situation can be debated.

Context

The word 'ambivalence' at the end of the first sentence in the paragraph, which you may not have known the meaning of at first reading, has, in fact, been defined by the answer:

> **ambivalence:** two opposing views, which have to be weighed up against each other

In other words, the **context** of the word – the rest of the sentence in which you find it – helps you to deduce its meaning.

The ability to deduce the meaning of a word from its context lies at the heart of our ability to understand language. As a baby, you learned to understand the word 'milk' because there actually was milk there in a cup or a bottle. Before you could read, you never looked up a word in the dictionary to see what a word meant. You knew its meaning because of the **context** in which you had heard the word. 'Mind the kerb'; 'go to sleep'; 'please bring me the book' are phrases you 'just knew' because of the place and the objects surrounding you.

It becomes more difficult later in life with abstract ideas, but there are still clues provided by the context. In the following example, 'voracious' is possibly a word you have not seen before.

> Since the 1990s, this disaster has seen the voracious global fishing system savage 90 per cent of the ocean's largest species – tuna, swordfish and sharks – bringing about an imminent end to the eco-system, the planet and the one billion people who rely on fish for protein.

From the context – in a sentence that includes words like 'disaster' and 'savage' – it is obvious that 'voracious' means something destructive which grabs 90 per cent of large fish.

If you deduced from this that 'voracious' involves vast consumption, you would be very close to its meaning which is 'extremely hungry' or 'desiring to devour'.

Summary

1 Questions may contain elements of all three aspects of your reading: understanding, analysis and evaluation.
2 These three skills are interdependent: analysis may help you to understand or vice versa. Evaluation should give you an overview of how understanding and analysis work together effectively.
3 The context (the sentence or paragraph surrounding an unfamiliar concept) can help you towards understanding it.

Understanding

Understanding the meaning of individual words or key phrases

Understanding is a basic skill that you need whenever you are asked in a question to **explain** something or to **identify** a point or points in the argument.

In both these situations you have to demonstrate that you understand the language of the passage, and to do that you have to understand the meaning of the words or phrases in the lines you are directed to look at. The following is a simple example.

> *The beneficial potential of new media is seldom given much publicity either. Research suggests that computer games can assist children's social and educational development.*

? Question

- Explain what needs to be more fully publicised.

Remember

Whether or not you are reminded explicitly to do so, you must always use your own words when you are offering an explanation.

Your answer has to show that you know what 'beneficial potential' means. The sentence that follows suggests that good results arise from the use of new media, so 'beneficial' must mean 'for the good' in some way, and 'potential' suggests that something 'can' happen or 'has the power' to happen – to bring about improved results in children's development.

Therefore your answer would read something like:

The fact that the new media have the possibility of being good for children's development needs to be given more publicity.

Or, more simply:

The new media offer the possibility of being good for children's development.

You have used the **context** of the sentence to help you towards the meaning of the phrase. This is exactly what you did with the word 'ambivalence' in the previous example on page 38.

Here is an example for you to try yourself from the same article as the previous one.

But today's concerns exist in the context of broader adult unease about the proliferation of technology, particularly in the home, and the challenge to adult authority that it represents. The majority of children in the UK now have their own laptop, tablet or smartphone. And they are frequently more competent navigators of the new media than their parents are.

(?) Question

- Explain what two things the adults are uneasy about. (**Answer (1)** on page 85.)

Summary 👍

1 Make sure that you tackle the difficult words in a phrase or sentence.
2 Remember that **context** is helpful and can help you to explain how you arrived at a particular meaning.

Identifying points

An important part of demonstrating your understanding of a passage or extract is to be able to recognise the evidence being provided to expand on the topic of a paragraph.

As you are expected to express these points in your own words, it is obvious that you must use the skills we have just dealt with in the previous section.

Here is a simple example:

Since the 1990s, this disaster has seen the voracious global fishing system savage 90 per cent of the ocean's largest species – tuna, swordfish and sharks – bringing about an imminent end to the eco-system, the planet and the one billion people who rely on fish for protein. And if we don't know much about fish in peril because we just don't particularly care – then why not? Is it because we 'must' eat fish for our 'essential' Omega 3, otherwise we'll be dead within weeks from nineteenth-century scurvy? Or because fish are Earth's own aliens, no-limbed spooky beings with amoebas for brains? Or because we've more important things to worry about, like unemployment?

? Question

- Identify three reasons why we don't care that we eat too much fish.

First you have to isolate the three reasons. The punctuation of a paragraph such as this often helps to clarify where one reason stops and the next begins. The three reasons follow the question '… we just don't particularly care – then why not?'

1 Is it because we 'must' eat fish for our 'essential' Omega 3, otherwise we'll be dead within weeks from nineteenth-century scurvy?
2 Or because fish are Earth's own aliens, no-limbed spooky beings with amoebas for brains?
3 Or because we have more important things to worry about, like unemployment?

We must now try to show that we understand the meaning of each.
1 Fish provides necessary items to supplement our diet so that we avoid illness.
2 Fish are not attractive animals so we don't care about them.
3 Other, more important, aspects of our real lives don't leave us any room to care about fish.

Try the following two examples:

Example 1

The informal curricular programme in schools is also changing and being given a larger role. Once we would have said this was to promote a rounded education, but now it also helps to hone the skills employers seek. Pursuing private passions through clubs – from the debating society to the magazine committee – has always been part of the lifeblood of a good school. A greater emphasis on civic engagement means volunteering your time: perhaps helping with art in a local primary school or helping with a riding scheme for the disabled. The new buzzword is 'entrepreneurship'. This autumn pupils will launch a charity shop. Run by students it will generate profits for a charity while giving its directors business experience.

? Question

- Identify three types of interests covered by a good informal curricular programme which are described in this paragraph. (**Answer (2)** on page 85.)

Hints & tips ★

The question asks why we don't care about eating too much fish. So the part of the paragraph that contains the answer will probably lie **after** that statement in the paragraph rather than before it – that is, in the last five lines of the paragraph. Follow this hint in Example 2 on page 42 when you come to it.

Hints & tips ★

In this case the finding of the three reasons is easy, as each is given a separate question. But to write them down, just as they are, lifted from the passage, would not gain any marks.

Example 2

> *The beneficial potential of new media is seldom given much publicity either. Research suggests that computer games can assist children's social and educational development. Young people are using technology to learn and connect with friends across the globe. Nor is the perception of computer games as unremittingly violent accurate, given that the majority of those aimed at children involve imaginative role play.*

(?) Question

- Identify three ways in which the new media benefit children's social and education development. (**Answer (3)** on page 85.)

> **Summary** 👍
>
> 1 Remember to use your own words where possible.
> 2 Use the sentences' structure and/or punctuation as a guide to isolating separate points.

Explaining developments

We have already looked at this idea in Chapter 2 in the sections on **Reading paragraphs** and **Reading sentences** on pages 34–36.

Questions that ask you to **explain** points rather than simply to **identify** them will involve this technique.

You will also need this technique for dealing with questions asking you to take a wider look at the passage(s). These questions could be about:
- the conclusion of an argument or
- the comparison between two passages or
- the necessity to summarise.

Links within a paragraph or sentence

Here, when you are dealing with a section of text, there will be links within the paragraph or sentence that show how the idea is developing.

In the previous section on **Identifying points** we dealt with simple addition: one point + second point + etc.

In an **explanation** of the development of an idea we are more likely to find a more complex relationship between the points. For example:
- an opposition – *but*
- a reason – *because*
- a solution – *therefore*.

Example 1

> *The findings of a survey of more than 2,100 adults suggest that fatherhood is becoming a mild form of depression for the modern-day man, with a grey cloud hanging over it. Many of these men thought of themselves as New Men (with all*

*the warm, sensitive emotional capacities that entails) **until** they became new fathers, which is **why** they are all the more disappointed when they fail to be the sort of dads they expected and hoped to be. The disappointment and feeling of failure **results** in men shutting down emotionally **because** they no longer have the old central role in their family and don't know what other role is available for them.*

(?) Question

- Explain how the idea that modern fatherhood is becoming a mild form of depression is developed.

Answer

- Their expectations of what they thought they would be like – ideal, bonded, caring – have not been realised. **Therefore** their disappointment has caused them to suppress their emotions **because** they don't know how to react.

Example 2
(The first part of the question has been answered for you.)

With nearly one million young people unemployed, few secondary-school age pupils could be unaware that their prospects are different from those of their parents. So in schools 'employability' is a focus in itself: academic qualifications count, but so do an understanding of the job market and the personal qualities of flexibility, imagination and adaptability. And careers education is a serious business. Diagnostic online profiling, subject choices and guidance on applying to university ensure that, in the final three years of school, the focus is on the long term.

(?) Question

- Identify the main idea in the topic sentence of this paragraph.

Answer

- Most secondary-school age pupils recognise that their prospects (for employment) are different from (worse than) those of their parents.

(?) Question

- Explain how the rest of the paragraph develops this idea. (**Answer (4)** on page 86.)

Links between paragraphs

In the context of the whole passage, or a major section of the passage, the tracing of development is important in helping you to recognise the major shifts in the writer's argument. Is the writer presenting conflicting points of view, building a cumulative one-sided case, showing a progression or presenting alternate paragraphs in opposition? Your ability to recognise what is going on is important for your overall understanding and evaluation of the passage(s).

Hints & tips ★

This requires more than just simple identification of points – you are asked to explain. Therefore, it is the relationship between the points that is important. In the answer, this is dealt with by using 'therefore' and 'because' – showing that there is a causal relationship between the two items: the two items don't exist in isolation from each other – there is a cause and therefore an effect.

Remember

Remember to answer questions using your own words.

We have already discussed linking in the chapter on discursive essays (page 6). This is just one example of how your ability to read and analyse other writers' prose helps you in your own attempts to write.

Example 1

Here is a simple example of helpful linking of an argument.

> **Two years ago**, this was my life: I worked in a converted warehouse in Hoxton, east London. It was a bright, young company; the work was brain-achingly demanding and we put in long hours. There were often drinks after work. Weekends consisted of hungover mornings in bed and longer lunches with friends. Resolutions to take more exercise and see more of the insides of theatres/museums were daily broken.

> **Yesterday**, at 5.30 a.m., I was to be found swaying to and fro in the dark, attempting to coax my toddler son back into his cot for another hour's sleep. His cries of 'sha' (lights) and 'poi' (porridge) were a bad omen and I soon conceded. On came the lights and we made our weary way downstairs. At 7 p.m., after almost 14 hours on the go, Jack went to bed. I washed up, watched telly, then went to bed early. This is my life.

> **Last week**, a report found that there are now in the region of 200,000 househusbands in this country: I am one of them …

The words in bold help you to find your way quickly through the writer's argument. In this case it is a really simple sequence.

The first two paragraphs show the contrast between his life then and his life now, leading up to the more general point, which is going to be covered in the information about 'last week's' report.

Example 2

In this next example, the linkage is not as obvious but it is effective in promoting the writer's argument. The important phrases are in bold.

> *You could sum up a year in a hundred different ways. Sport, weather, births, deaths, affairs of state, or the fortunes of a single life. If you are allowed only one choice, though, which headline sticks? As December 2013 descended into hard rain and hail, there was this:* **'Fivefold increase in users of food banks and soup kitchens.'**
>
> *If you didn't pause over* **that statement,** *you are either very young or very lucky. In most of my existence the idea of soup kitchens was confined to grainy photographs from bygone days, or to seasonal appeals for the destitute. Now it is commonplace.* **What was once troubling passes for normal.**
>
> **It has become normal with astonishing speed.** *Wages are depressed while bills rise ever upward. Pensions and savings descend to the level of a lottery. Education, once the route to security, has left us with legions of well-read casual labourers. For those not granted even that promise there is the zero hours contract, the bedroom tax, the abolition of any right to social security and the stigma of poverty.*

Look at how the linking helps you to follow the argument.

The link between the first paragraph and the second is the phrase 'If you didn't pause over that statement …' The words 'that statement' take you back to the previous sentence about 'soup kitchens', and the rest of the paragraph that follows deals with the idea of 'soup kitchens' in the past and in the present.

The link between the second and the third paragraph is contained in the sentence 'It has become normal with astonishing speed'. The word 'normal' picks up the idea of the 'normalisation' of the drastic situation talked of in the paragraph about soup kitchens and the 'astonishing speed' looks forward to what is described in the rest of the third paragraph about the problems caused by the escalation of the present economic situation.

The development of the argument can be traced though the three paragraphs as follows:
1 The rise of soup kitchens is the most important headline of the year.
2 Soup kitchens were a thing of the past, a bad memory, but now they are considered normal again.
3 This has all happened very quickly because of the dire economic situation.

Mastering this skill allows you to pinpoint the important stages in the writer's argument.

Hints & tips

You may not be asked a question explicitly about linkage, but it is important that you can see this technique in operation as it will help you to deal with the second passage in the exam paper.

Here is an example for you to tackle yourself.

Example 3

> *The stakes have never been higher, scientists said. The oceans are becoming increasingly important to global food security. Each year more than a million commercial fishing vessels extract more than 80 million metric tonnes of fish and seafood from the ocean. Up to three billion people rely on the sea for a large share of their protein, especially in the developing world.*
>
> *Those demands are only projected to grow. 'If you look at where food security has to go between now and 2030 we have to start looking at the ocean. We have to start looking at the proteins coming from the sea,' said Valerie Hickey, an environmental scientist at the World Bank.*
>
> *That makes it all the more crucial to crack down on illegal and unregulated fishing, which is sabotaging efforts to build sustainable seafood industries. Two-thirds of the fish taken on the high seas are from stocks that are already dangerous depleted – far more so than in those parts of the ocean that lie within 200 miles of the shore and are under direct national control.*

? Question

- Identify the links in the writer's argument. (**Answer (5)** on page 86.)

(**Answer (5)** on page 86.)

Summary 👍

1 When you are asked to explain, it means you have to do more than just identify.
2 Linking words and phrases (and sentences) help to signpost stages in the writer's thought, and therefore help your explanation.
3 Remember it is still important to put as much of your answer as you can in your own words.

Hints & tips ⭐

Look out for repetition of words or ideas, and watch for the words that create stages in the argument — the signposts mentioned on page 6.

Use of examples/illustrations and anecdotes

Writers often use examples and anecdotes to clarify abstract points in their argument. This helps the reader because it takes the abstract idea and presents it in human terms. It is often why serious articles about, for example, political dilemmas use what are called 'human interest' stories. Such articles are attempting to clarify a situation by using the description of an actual human experience, and they are often trying to engage your sympathies on a personal as well as an intellectual level.

Example 1

> I visited a Trussell Trust foodbank this week, in Hackney in East London, no more than a three-minute walk from a pleasant green complete with upmarket cafés and a specialist Italian deli. It is a sight at once heartening and shaming. Heartening because it is good to see that people are still willing to give up time, money and effort to care with great sensitivity and respect for those they have never met. Shaming because, in global terms, 'we are a wealthy country', and in a wealthy country people should not go hungry.
>
> The pity of it is inescapable. I saw a man take home a couple of carrier bags filled with the most basic kind of basics: tinned sausages, a can of soup, a packet of pasta. All decent enough, each allocation calculated for balance by nutritionists. Except that you and I would not want to live on that for three days, which is how long it has to last.

In this example the abstract ideas of 'shame' and 'in a wealthy country people should not grow hungry' are given more emotional impact by the author's description of a real person who is reduced to plastic bags of 'basics'. It induces the 'pity' he is trying to raise in his readers.

Example 2

> Without doubt we humans are changing, just as we changed centuries ago with the print revolution. But research into the effects of new technology has always been contradictory.
>
> People once fretted over what the telephone and the radio would do to us. In 1835, the American Annals of Education declared that 'the perpetual reading' of novels 'inevitably operates to exclude thought and, in the youthful mind, to stint the opening mental faculties, by favouring unequal development: no-one can have time for reflection, who reads at this rapid rate'.

(?) Question

- This example works in the same way as the previous one. Comment on its effectiveness. (**Answer (6)** on page 86.)

Example 3

This anecdote occurs in an article criticising the way in which emails and mobile phones have spread through all aspects of our lives. The writer does not use either of these.

> *The only time I might conceivably have needed a mobile phone outside the house was when I once turned my car over in the Irish mountains and was trapped inside the vehicle for a while. When a passer-by did finally try to use a phone, however, it didn't work, since the mountains were too high. Hanging upside down like a gigantic bat, my chest crushed painfully against the airbag, I felt quietly vindicated.*

(?) Question

- Explain how this anecdote helps to support the writer's stance about mobile phones. (**Answer (7)** on page 86.)

Effectiveness of a conclusion

This kind of question is quite commonly used to check that you have followed the argument of the paragraph, or – more commonly – a whole passage, and that you can appreciate the writer's skill in reaching an effective conclusion.

A good conclusion to an article normally achieves one, or both, of the following:

1 It should tie up the writer's argument (the ideas), making clear his or her stance/point of view
2 It should relate to the rest of the article, by reminding us of important points, by choice of language or by structural techniques.

Although the following piece (only 331 words) is shorter than passages you will get in the exam, it is enough to illustrate the idea of an effective conclusion.

Example 1

Hunger for success

> *It is interesting to see a new Department for Education study urging universities to consider lowering entry requirements for state-school pupils. It argues that when state-educated pupils have the same grades as those educated at fee-paying schools, on average they go on to attain better degrees, and are also less likely to drop out.*

> *These state-school students have to fight against unfair odds to get into universities, a battle that these days incorporates everything from limited educational opportunities and lack of financial*

support to huge fees and loans. The whole process looks unfair, exhausting and economically terrifying, and that's even when everything goes to plan. Saying that, what this study suggests is that, given half a chance, many students from the fabled 'wrong side of town' have what it takes to excel at university level, even to surpass some of their more privileged peers. It would appear that the determination required to keep hacking away, fighting through the thickets and briars of a disadvantaged start, the intelligence and strong will that keeps a person focused and on track stays with them during their university years.

Could this be where the disadvantaged have a bizarre kind of advantage? For all the love and good intentions that may be around them, the support and opportunities too often aren't – so they have no choice but to be self-starting, self-motivated, their own raw version of self-made.

Take this attitude into a university setting, where self-reliance is king, and it becomes akin to having a superpower. Getting bored, becoming demotivated, giving up, dropping out – to the disadvantaged, self-made university student, these options would be unthinkable.

The thought that, once at university, such students tend not only to do well, but disproportionately so, is encouraging – which in turn lends weight to the argument for helping more of them do likewise, by the simple act of lowering university requirements to a fair and realistic level. Far from being reverse discrimination, this would be anti-discrimination, ultimately benefiting all.

⑦ Question

- Evaluate the final paragraph's effectiveness as a conclusion to the article.

Answer

- The last paragraph provides an effective conclusion to the ideas of the passage as it takes into account the two main ideas of the passage: that entry to university education is unfair to state-educated pupils (although there might ultimately be some advantage in this for the them); and that the system ought to be reformed to get rid of the inequalities.
- The last sentence is particularly effective in summing up in a few words the fairness of a reformed system, with the climax being the notion that it would benefit everyone.

This answer has looked mainly at ideas, but the technique of building to a climax in the last sentence is also mentioned.

Example 2

I am not connected

I shall soon be the only EMV (email virgin) left in the country. I have never sent an email, though I've occasionally cheated and asked my teenage son to do so for me. Nor have I ever used the internet. I am no more capable of going online than I am of getting to Saturn. I don't know how to text. I do have a mobile phone, but it's immobile. I never take it out of the house, for fear of triggering some ridiculous trend in which a horde of people march down the street bawling into these sinister little gadgets. If you allowed people to use mobile phones in public, you might end up being forced to listen to them on trains and in cafés, asking noisily whether the invoices have arrived. The prospect is too appalling to contemplate. The only time I might conceivably have needed a mobile phone outside the house was when I once turned my car over in the Irish mountains and was trapped inside the vehicle for a while. When a passer-by did finally try to use a phone, however, it didn't work, since the mountains were too high. Hanging upside down like a gigantic bat, my chest crushed painfully against the airbag, I felt quietly vindicated.

Nowadays, however, protest is most definitely what my email virginity has become. I am living proof that all this frenetic, mostly vacuous, communication is quite superfluous. We all survived without it before it started, and I personally have survived without it ever since. If people really want to contact me they write. If they can't be bothered, or have forgotten how to do it, that's their problem.

❓ Question

- Explain how the last paragraph makes an effective conclusion to the article. (**Answer (8)** on page 86.)

(**Answer (8)** on page 86.)

> ### *Hints & tips* ⭐
>
> *Look for repetition in the last paragraph of words, phrases or imagery that have occurred earlier in the passage — often at the very beginning. Sometimes the title or heading of the passage is echoed in the conclusion.*

Summary 👍

1 Look at how the ideas have been followed through to the ending, clarifying the writer's stance or point of view.
2 Consider the techniques the writer uses to emphasise his or her stance, or to provide a climax to or a final twist in the article.

Analysis

We have seen already how understanding, analysis and evaluation are inextricably mixed together, but on some occasions you will be asked to comment on or evaluate the effectiveness of certain features or techniques employed by the writer.

There are several ways in which you could be asked to approach these questions. For example:

- By referring to at least one example, analyse how the writer's use of imagery …
- By referring to examples, analyse how the writer's use of word choice and sentence structure …
- By referring to at least two features of language, analyse … You should refer in your answer to such features as sentence structure, word choice, tone …
- By referring to at least two features of language, analyse …

In the first case, you have no choice, you have to analyse the feature mentioned – in this case, imagery.

In the second case, you have no choice, you have to analyse the features mentioned – in this case, word choice and sentence structure. This is a **closed** list – you can't choose anything else.

In the third case, you can analyse any feature you think is effective. The list you are given is an **open** list – you may accept the suggestions offered to you, but you could choose any language feature you think is effective.

In the fourth case, you can again choose any language feature you think is effective, but you are given no support, so you should have a 'tick list' in your head to remind you of the kind of features you might be looking for.

In the following section we are going to look at the following items on that 'tick list' which you will find useful in answering such questions:

1 word choice
2 imagery
3 sentence structure
4 tone.

Word choice

This is really a very simple technique to get to grips with. The question you have to ask yourself is **why** a writer has chosen one particular word to describe someone or something, rather than any of the other words that have a similar meaning. English is a rich language – it has twice the vocabulary of French, for example – and has many **synonyms** (words of the same meaning). Purists in language will tell you that there is no such thing as a synonym – and they are right – but for our purposes we will stick with the common definition.

Take 'friendly', 'chummy' and 'comradely'. All three of these could describe a comfortable relationship. They have the same 'meaning'. The technical word for this is **denotation**. Any English speaker would recognise the kind of person being described.

But there is a difference between the effect of each of the three words. Each of them *implies* something different about the relationship. This further implication is technically called **connotation**.

The table below shows the denotations and connotations of the three words.

Word	Denotation	Connotation
Friendly	Close relationship	A fairly neutral description of people who find pleasure in each other's company.
Chummy	Close relationship	Suggests an intimacy shared between two people who are close and comfortable in each other's company, perhaps for a long time – since childhood maybe.
Comradely	Close relationship	Suggests a closeness coming from mutual support – possibly belonging to a team or an organisation.

Writers are careful in their choice of words – it is their profession, after all. We should do them the honour of appreciating the effects their choices have on us. Connotations are sometimes hard to pin down – you know what effect the words have, but you can't quite explain it. The larger the vocabulary you have, the more likely it is that you can find the words you need to describe the connotations, and that goes back to the amount you read or listen to. Constant practice is the best way.

Let's look again at one of the examples used at the start of this chapter to explore the connotations of words.

Hints & tips

You should skip the denotation stage in your comment on word choice – it is self-evident and can confuse an otherwise good answer. What is important is the connotation you identify to show the effect of the choice of that particular word. For example, you could say '"comradely" suggests a supporting friendship among a group of people – possibly in the same organisation'. You do not have to say what the denotation is.

Example 1

> And yet our panic about childhood betrays a deep ambivalence, too. Our children are in danger, fattened on fast food, corrupted by commerce, traumatised by testing. And, at the same time, other children are dangerous, malevolent beneath hooded tops, chaotic in the classroom, perilous on the pavements. Before we can have a sensible debate on child-rearing, we need to unpick which of our anxieties truly reflects the reality of the situation.

The most obvious examples of the writer choosing words to make an effect are the ones where she is talking about the negative views of childhood. The list of possibilities is quite extensive.

- '**fattened**' suggests that the children are likely to become obese, almost like pigs which are 'fattened' especially for market.
- '**fast food**' suggests cheap, not particularly nutritious food, not prepared with care and therefore not healthy.
- '**corrupted**' – the idea of corruption is strong, as if the children are part of the criminal world already.

- '**commerce**' possibly suggests that they are part of a society that buys and sells anything for profit.
- '**traumatised**' suggests that the children have actually been wounded, perhaps not physically, but certainly mentally.
- '**testing**' suggests an unpleasant experience with scary exams.
- '**malevolent**' suggests that children can be seen almost as bad spirits, out to cause harm deliberately.
- '**hooded**' suggests something hidden, and therefore mysterious, threatening and dangerous.

> **Hints & tips** ★
>
> The word 'suggests' is used in these answers to show that you are moving from the reference (for which you get no marks) to the connotative area of the word you have chosen to deal with.

> **Hints & tips** ★
>
> You would not choose anything like this number of words for comment. The easiest to deal with are probably 'fattened', 'corrupted', 'traumatised' and 'hooded'. You should take note of the number of marks available for your answer and assume that you stand a chance of making at least 1 mark for each comment. Remember that you gain no marks for simply quoting the word itself. The mark is in the comment.

Now look at the following example and answer the question that follows.

Example 2

> *There's also the matter of not being bothered enough to think of anything else to eat in the face of a sumptuously juicy salmon steak fizzing away under the grill, to be served with a drizzle of virgin olive oil and a splash of the zingiest lemon – yum! For me, a world without fish is a world where there's nowt for tea. I write as someone who eats fish three times a week, who hasn't eaten meat since 1983 and has been resolutely adolescent on the subject ever since.*

(?) Question

- Analyse how the writer, by her word choice, makes her eating of fish sound attractive. (**Answer (9)** on pages 86–87.)

> **Hints & tips** ★
>
> This question is not quite typical of the question you may actually be asked in the exam. It would be more usual to find 'word choice' as one of a number of techniques you are offered for comment. You could also comment on 'word choice' in an answer to a question asking you to analyse the language of a particular sentence or paragraph.
>
> 'Language' covers a number of techniques besides word choice, including imagery, sentence structure and tone, which will be discussed in the rest of this section on Analysis.

Now look at the following example:

Example 3

> *It is difficult being a househusband; certainly more difficult than I had imagined. The practical aspects of parenting – naps, meals, baths, bedtimes – are well established. None of it is the least bit difficult, once you know how. But a lot of it is boring. And the hours … they start when it's dark and cold, and they last for an unreasonable amount of time. There is little time to yourself; no time for mulling over your emails, or surfing the web, or popping out for some pleasure shopping. There's no breakfast and a shower before work. You live and sleep on the shop floor.*

⑦ Question

- By referring to at least two examples, analyse how the writer gives the impression that being a househusband is time-consuming. (**Answer (10)** on page 87.)

Summary 👍

1 The more extensive your vocabulary, the more easily will you be able to express the connotations of the words you choose to examine.
2 The more you read, the more you will extend your vocabulary.

Imagery

Imagery can refer to pictures or photographs. It is also a technical term used in the analysis of language. The following passage, although it paints a picture and is very descriptive, does not contain any imagery. You could make valid comments on the word choice, but not on imagery.

> *Seven great swans flew overhead, snow-plumaged travellers from the far north who knew the glacial winds of the tundra and the sunny waters of Andalusia. The sun shone on the snow white heads as they swept across the blue-arched sky; then they were gone, with a far carrying swoosh of wings. They had passed over a Glasgow suburb only fifteen minutes before, flying high and strong in the familiar cold, unheard, unseen, eager to splash and dip their beaks in the cold water of the loch beyond Laverock Knowe.*

Imagery in its technical sense has many divisions, but here we are concerned with the following more common ones:

- simile
- metaphor
- personification
- symbolism.

Simile

This is perhaps the easiest to spot because it always has a 'like' or an 'as', but it is not necessarily easy to explain. Take this very simple, rather clichéd, example.

Example 1

> *The messenger ran like the wind.*

If you were asked to analyse the effect of this simile, you could say:

Answer

- The simile gives the impression of the messenger's speed, as the wind is seen as a powerful force that can reach great speeds.

An answer such as 'the messenger runs very fast' would only be giving the meaning of the phrase, not its effect.

In the next extract, taken from a passage about girls and sport, there are two examples of simile, both of which help us to visualise a situation, i.e. they transmit to us an image, making the writer's point more effective.

Example 2

> *It happened overnight. One minute, I was flying down the wing like a character out of 'Bunty'*, my only worry in life that I would lose control of the ball and thus let down our captain Caroline 'Caz' Johnson, a girl who seriously demanded to be impressed. The next, I was a 'Jackie'** photo-strip, obsessed with frosted lipstick and whether my hair looked like Siobhan's out of 'Bananarama'.*
>
> *After this, there was no way back. Reluctant to run or indeed make sudden movements of any kind, I was soon dropped from the hockey team. PE lessons, meanwhile, became a convoluted exercise in avoidance – and not only for me. The slothfulness spread among us girls like a contagion. Cross-country runs began with a truculent jog until we were out of sight of the teachers, at which point we would repair to the nearest newsagent for sweets and a Coke.*

* 'Bunty' was a magazine for girls at the pre-teen stage – now out of print.

** 'Jackie' was a photo-magazine for teenage girls – also now out of print.

The two similes in this paragraph are:
- 'I was flying down the wing like a character out of 'Bunty''.
- 'The slothfulness spread among us girls like a contagion.'
- 'I was flying down the wing like a character out of 'Bunty'' is a simile in which the writer compares herself to a character out of 'Bunty' – suggesting that her role models then were the kind of sporty heroines to be found in a magazine such as 'Bunty', which was aimed at pre-teen girls.

? Question

- Comment on the second simile about 'slothfulness'. (**Answer (11)** on page 87.)

Example 3

> *Last week, a report found that there are now in the region of 200,000 househusbands in this country: I am one of them. Like blue whales, we rarely meet and when we do, we cluster. I know about eight other househusbands, although, to be pedantic about it, most of them are part-timers, splitting the domestic stuff with their partners. And part-time is not full-time; there is a profound difference. I have abandoned my career to raise our son and, perhaps one day, his sibling. When I fill in forms now, under occupation I write 'househusband'.*

(?) Question

- Analyse how the simile in this paragraph helps to emphasise the numbers of househusbands. (**Answer (12)** on page 87.)

Metaphor

A metaphor is the most powerful (and magical) device in the language. If you can learn to appreciate its strength and beauty, it doesn't really matter whether you pass the exam or not – you are a more enlightened person!

Metaphor goes one step further than simile:
- **Simile** says something is *like* something – her home is like a prison.
- **Metaphor** says something *is* something – her home is a prison.

The first of these statements can be true – her home has bolts and bars, high fences, etc.

The second of these statements is not actually true – her home is not one of Her Majesty's prison buildings. But it suggests that some attributes of both home and prison are shared. Some of the connotations of prison are possibly isolation, oppression, being trapped – not necessarily just physical bolts and bars. The metaphor fuses the concepts of 'prison' and 'home' together to make an entirely new concept. It is more powerful than the simile because it opens up many more possibilities – psychological as well as physical. It really creates a new concept – a prison/home.

Think about the following metaphor:

> *In the wind the men clung on to the big, black, circular birds of their umbrellas.*

The two concepts of 'big, black birds' and '(black) umbrellas' are being compared and condensed into a new visual concept suggesting, among other things, that the umbrellas are now animate beings and have a life of their own. The metaphor exists in the overlap between the two connotational areas – the one surrounding 'black birds' and the one surrounding 'umbrellas'.

The process can be illustrated in graphic form in a Venn diagram – it helps some people whose mind works spatially, rather than abstractly.

Hints & tips ★

A number of the questions throughout the Analysis section of this book are much narrower and more specific than the questions you may get in the exam. In a typical exam question, you might be asked specifically about word choice or imagery, etc.; but it is equally likely that the question would ask 'by referring to at least two features of language …' It is on these occasions that you have to remind yourself of the features of language discussed here.

CONNOTATIONAL IDEAS

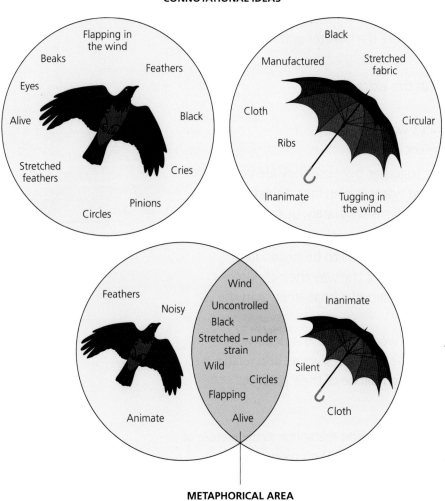

METAPHORICAL AREA

Try disentangling the following example – which is a mixture of simile and metaphor – just for fun!

The umbrella suddenly bellied out, the spokes tore through the soaking cover; the wind danced its tatters; it wrangled above us in the wind like a ruined mathematical bird. We tried to tug it down: an unseen new spoke sprang through its ragged ribs.

The following example is a more typical one to try. It is from an article about the difficulties facing children of the twenty-first century.

Example 1

But that's not how it is for my kids, and it's not how it is for most kids these days, either: because most of us parents are still largely in control, still mostly rowing our boats, still on the whole steering our children through life's waters and making sure they know what matters in life.

Being a kid has never been so good; I feel excited with my children, and for my children, that they're growing up where they are, and when they are: and I believe in them, and in their generation.

As far as I can see, there's a lot more honey than poison in the cocktail that is childhood in the twenty-first century: and my kids, and all the other kids I know, are the sweeter and more promising for it.

There are a number of metaphors in this extract:

- rowing our boats
- steering our children through life's waters
- more honey than poison in the cocktail.

The first two of these could be put together, because they are both concerned with the idea of boats and water. It is, in fact, an **extended metaphor**. But you can deal with the items separately, or together.

The metaphor 'rowing our boats … steering our children through life's waters' pictures life as being like a sea that needs to be negotiated. It emphasises the parents being in control of the way their children are growing up through life, just as a captain of a boat steers it in the right direction.

This analysis shows how the metaphor works, because it deals with the **figurative** element, the image of the sea/boats/water, and relates it to children's **literal** growing up under the guidance of their parents.

? Question

- Analyse the contribution of the honey/poison metaphor to the picture of twenty-first century children's lives. (**Answer (13)** on page 87.)

Hints & tips ★

In dealing with metaphors, you should:

✓ *Show how the words used metaphorically help to enlarge or refine your idea of what is being described (a house, a bat, a child's life).*

✓ *Show the link between the literal (or denotational) meaning of the words used in the metaphor (prison, bits of umbrella, life's waters) and the figurative effect — caused among other things by the fusing of the two concepts.*

Here is another example from a different article on the difficulties facing children of the twenty-first century.

Example 2

Childhood has always been a disputed territory, its true geography quickly forgotten as we grow older, replaced by an adult-imagined universe. But there appears to be a growing consensus that childhood today is in a peculiarly parlous state.

? Question

- Analyse the writer's use of imagery in these lines. (**Answer (14)** on pages 87–88.)

Examples 3 and 4 (below) are from the passage about sustainable fishing.

Example 3

No, we don't care about fish because we don't know anything about fish or how they came to be sizzling on our plates. Plundering shoals in supermarkets, we are ill-informed innocents at best, consumptive zombies at worst: inadvertently slicing the kitchen knife through the cast of Finding Nemo in front of our weeping children, who may never see their own offspring shriek like seagulls at a gigantic skate's rectangular mouth grimacing through an aquarium wall.

? Question

- Analyse how the imagery in this paragraph helps the writer to make her point effectively. (**Answer (15)** on page 88.)

Example 4

Since the 1990s, this disaster has seen the voracious global fishing system savage 90 per cent of the ocean's largest species – tuna, swordfish and sharks – bringing about an imminent end to the eco-system, the planet and the one billion people who rely on fish for protein.

? Question

- Analyse the imagery in this paragraph. (**Answer (16)** on page 88.)

Summary 👍

1 Identify or quote the metaphor you are dealing with.
2 Show how the literal and the figurative come together to create an effect.
3 Say what the effect is.

Personification

Personification is really just another kind of metaphor (a 'subset' for those who are mathematically inclined). In personification, some thing or animal is given human attributes. For example, 'The river babbled happily, chuckling over the stones', is a simple use of personification. What is gained by using this sentence rather than simply 'The river flowed over the stones making small noises'? The river, not being a person, cannot either 'babble happily' or 'chuckle' (these being human actions) – but the feeling of happiness and serenity (which are among the connotations of the words) is transferred to the scene by regarding the river as a friendly entity.

Look at the first example, which is the conclusion to the article used on page 55 on girls and sport.

Example 1

> *They need to transmit their excitement, their satisfaction, their sense of liberation and empowerment.*
>
> *When I think back to the 'Bananarama' days, my hair crisp with Sun-In and Wella gel, it is this flimsiness that pains me most, the sense that I would only be noticed, be found attractive, if I was a blonde smile in stretch jeans. I can't deny that in my nylon hockey skirt and clumpy studded boots, my knees covered in mud and my sweaty fringe in my eyes, I felt that I looked too substantial, too challenging. And that feeling stayed with me for years, long after my hockey stick had been laid to rest in the attic.*
>
> *How I wish I'd known then what I know now, which is that energy, zest and, above all, strength are twice as attractive as a pampered skin and at least three times as enduring.*

⑦ Question

- One example of imagery is 'a blonde smile in stretch jeans'. Comment on this metaphor for yourself. (**Answer (17)** on page 88.)

The other example of imagery – 'long after my hockey stick had been laid to rest' – can be dealt with as a metaphor. It is also an example of personification. It doesn't matter which heading you analyse it under – either would be possible – but because this section is on personification, the answer here deals with it as personification.

The hockey stick is being seen as an animate object – a human being – which is 'laid to rest' in the way that you would bury a dead relative.

It suggests that the hockey stick was an old friend, but it had come to the end of its useful life, and was 'buried' in the attic. It is effective in showing how the writer looks back on her sporting life with some affection, and perhaps wishes that she had not so easily given up hockey.

This example is from an article about food phonies and their love of gastroculture.

Example 2

Gastroculture has a lot to answer for. It has monopolised television schedules. It has spawned live events and even muscled its way into music festivals via gourmet food trucks and VIP dining tickets.

(?) Question

- In what way does personification in this paragraph help promote the writer's critical view of gastroculture? (**Answer (18)** on page 88.)

Symbolism

This concept is related to imagery, but has a much wider significance and a more general application – not just in language, but in art, film and collective culture.

Thus symbols do not have to have a context in a piece of writing to be effective. A red rose is a symbol, whether it is a physical rose, a virtual rose, a drawing or a photograph of a rose, or the use of the word 'rose'. In the culture of Western Europe it is recognised as a symbol for love.

Literary symbolism, whether in novel, short story, film or a piece of journalism, is created by the writer specifically to carry an attitude, an

Hints & tips ⭐

A number of the questions throughout the Analysis section of this book are much narrower and more specific than the questions you may get in the exam. In a typical exam question, you might be asked specifically about word choice or imagery, etc.; but it is equally likely that the question would ask 'by referring to at least two features of language...' It is on these occasions that you have to remind yourself of the features of language discussed here.

emotion or a concept. In *The Cone-Gatherers* the tree and its disease becomes symbolic of Duror's descent into evil. In *Sunset Song*, the standing stones become symbolic of the old ways, Scotland, the land …

In a short article or extract it is not often possible to develop anything of a symbolic nature, but the article we have already looked at on househusbands offers a small example.

Example 1

(Second paragraph of the article on househusbands.)

> *Yesterday, at 5.30 a.m., I was to be found swaying to and fro in the dark, attempting to coax my toddler son back into his cot for another hour's sleep. His cries of 'sha' (lights) and 'poi' (porridge) were a bad omen and I soon conceded. On came the lights and we made our weary way downstairs.*

(And this is the conclusion.)

> *We spend nearly every waking hour together, yet when I'm not with him I miss him. I know what 'poi' and 'sha' mean. Above all, I know in every bone of my body that I will never regret this. I will not lie on my deathbed and think, oh, how I wish I'd spent less time with my son.*

? Question

- What effect does the writer create by his use of the repeated words 'poi' and 'sha' in this article?

Answer

- It is probably true to say that 'poi' and 'sha' have become symbolic of his understanding relationship with his son. It is effective in showing the depth of emotion contained in the intimate domestic detail the symbol is based on.

Sentence structure

Questions on sentence structure require more than just giving the meaning of the sentence. You must talk about the effect of the structure. Does it:
- clarify?
- dramatise?
- balance/contrast ideas?
- shock?

In order to tackle these sentences you should be thinking of at least four possibilities:
1 punctuation
2 length of sentence
3 use of climax or anti-climax
4 repetition (both in sentences and in other contexts).

Hints & tips

You should learn this list so that you can apply each to any sentence structure you are asked about: it is very likely that one of these techniques will be used in the extract.

Punctuation

You should know the various functions of the main punctuation marks in English:

- full stop (.)
- comma (,)
- semi-colon (;)
- colon (:)
- exclamation mark (!)
- question mark (?)
- inverted commas ('x').

The main purpose of punctuation is to help the reader to understand the sentence. Some of the possible uses are:

- Full stops tell you when one point has been finished.
- An exclamation mark will help you to recognise the tone of a sentence.
- A colon may signal an explanation which you need.
- Semi-colons may provide you with a balancing point in a sentence, either a parallel or a contrast.
- Brackets, pairs of dashes and pairs of commas may indicate a parenthesis.
- Inverted commas may mean quotation, or a title, or they may cast doubt on the truthfulness of the words they highlight.

Example 1

> For Rosie and her pals, friendship is hugely important: she and her little gang meet every week or so at someone's house for a pizza and a DVD (another encounter with the small screen) but, hey, they love it. They chat. They giggle. They enjoy one another's company. They can communicate, and communicate well. They make allowances for one another. They share a joke.

Punctuation of these sentences helps to clarify the writer's attitude to her daughter and her friends.

In the first sentence:

- The colon after 'friendship is hugely important' introduces an example of how that friendship works.
- The parenthesis reminds us of the part of the article, earlier in the passage, that suggests that children spend too long with computers and phones.
- The informality of the structure 'but, hey, they love it' is appropriate for a paragraph describing children's behaviour – it echoes their methods of communication.
- The series of short sentences all beginning with 'They' shows how cooperatively they work together.
- The repetition of the word 'communicate' makes that the most important benefit they share.

Obviously you would not be expected to give such a lengthy answer as this, but in this short passage there are several of the common usages of punctuation.

Hints & tips ★

A few common errors to do with punctuation:

- Commas do not, on their own, 'do' anything. They may help to mark out something that is already happening in a sentence.
- A single dash may create a pause or allow the addition of an important or dramatic idea – but one dash is not a parenthesis. A parenthesis requires a pair of something: dashes, commas or brackets.

Example 2

> *'Imagine a world without fish.' So runs the simple tag-line for
> The End of the Line, a documentary film about fish and how
> there literally won't be any left in 2048 due to over-fishing and all
> of its deadly friends: industry ruthlessness, merciless profiteering,
> governmental short-sightedness, consumer apathy, general
> ignorance and outright contempt for the spectrum of marine life
> by the majority of human beings.*

The colon after 'all of its deadly friends' introduces a list of the 'deadly friends' of over-fishing. The length of the list shows how many and varied are the enemies of fish stocks, and how likely they are in combination to end up in 'a world without fish' – the important topic sentence. The list builds up to a climax, saving the most important item for last, and the last item is much longer than the rest – 'general ignorance and outright contempt for the spectrum of marine life by the majority of human beings'. Basically the list ends up accusing the reader of being responsible for the depletion of fish stocks.

Example 3

> *Employment is one thing; finding fulfilment and making a
> worthwhile contribution to society is another. Whatever their
> immediate job prospects, and the difficulties that they will face,
> I think that the young people I meet are imaginative, tenacious,
> versatile and well-grounded. If our future is in their hands, then I
> am optimistic.*

? Question

- Analyse the effect of punctuation in these lines in contributing to the strength of this concluding paragraph. (**Answer (19)** on page 88.)

Hints & tips ★

You should identify the sentence you are writing about. Sometimes there are two lists quite close together in the passage, so to avoid confusion, use quotes. You don't need to quote the whole sentence or list – the line reference will do, or the opening and closing words.

Lists are easy to identify, but you must say what the effect of the list is – does it climax in something exciting, for example? Or does it suggest monotonous sameness? Or does it suggest an infinity or an infinite variety of items?

Sentence length

Really there are only two possible comments to make – either the sentence is 'long' or it is 'short'.

Commenting on a sentence's great length on its own is very unlikely to be helpful: there will be more important features, possibly statement and explanation or expansion; parenthetical detail marked by brackets or dashes; lengthy informative lists – the length of the sentence is purely incidental.

A short sentence is more likely to create an obvious effect in a piece of writing than a long one. A short sentence can be:

- dramatic
- declarative
- climactic
- summative.

In each case, a short sentence can be effective in serving the writer's purposes.

Example 1

> *The other day I was kicked out of a ladies' lavatory.*

(The rest of the article discusses the problems caused for a parent who is of the opposite sex from his young child, and which public lavatory to use.)

Obviously this is an example of a dramatic short sentence, its effect being to jolt us into reading what comes next.

Example 2

> *Whatever their immediate job prospects, and the difficulties that they will face, I think that the young people I meet are imaginative, tenacious, versatile and well-grounded. If our future is in their hands, then I am optimistic.*

The last short sentence 'If our … optimistic' could be described as 'declarative': it makes a strong statement which is sure of its ground and does not expect any opposition.

Example 3

> *Still, the shame is bearable if the alternative is you or your family going hungry. What has become of us, when that is the choice we offer our fellow citizens: dignity or food? And this in our wealthy, wealthy country.*

The last short sentence 'And … country' provides a climax to the writer's disapproval of food banks.

Starting the sentence with 'And' emphasises the importance of what the writer is saying. He doesn't just tack it on to the previous sentence in what would be considered a more conventionally 'correct' way. By separating it from its parent sentence the writer forces us to take note of it.

Example 4

> *Yesterday, at 5.30 a.m., I was to be found swaying to and fro in*
> *the dark, attempting to coax my toddler son back into his cot*
> *for another hour's sleep… At 7 p.m., after almost 14 hours on*
> *the go, Jack went to bed. I washed up, watched telly, then went*
> *to bed early. This is my life.*

The final short sentence 'This is my life' is summative – it parcels all the
long hours he has spent looking after his son into one small phrase that
contains it all. The sentence could be described also as anti-climactic, or
perhaps even climactic, depending on how you feel about children.

Use of climax and anti-climax

These features are fairly self-explanatory. All that you have to remember is
that they present possible areas for comment on sentence structure.

You may be asked specifically to comment on climax or anti-climax, but
you should be aware that, when asked to comment on the effectiveness
of a sentence, this is a technique worth looking for because its effect is
usually fairly easy to describe. The specific word or phrase could be the
last item in a list, the last sentence or phrase in a sequence or the last
sentence or phrase in a paragraph.

- Example 2 on page 64 shows how climax operates in a list.
- Example 4 above shows the climax of a paragraph.
- Example 3 on page 64 gives an example of climax at the end of an article.

Repetition

Although we are dealing with this under sentence structure, repetition can be
effective in many structures. It is not exclusively a feature within a **sentence**. It
can be found in **paragraphs** or **complete articles**.

Repetition in the structure of a paragraph

Look at this example from an article entitled 'Have we poisoned
childhood?'

Example

> *Too much TV. Bombarded with adverts. Too scared*
> *to go outside. Too much fat and sugar. Easily accessed*
> *internet pornography. Pressure at school. Mum and Dad*
> *both at work. Too many computer games. Too many*
> *celebrities to copy, or pity, or aspire to. Too much stuff.*
> *Endless piles of stuff.*

In this paragraph the repetition of 'Too' throughout is effective in
indicating all the 'excess' heaped on the twenty-first-century child.

Repetition in the structure of a whole article

Example

(Second paragraph in the article.)

> *So, presumably, we are nightmare parents, raising a nightmare generation on a poisonous cocktail of junk food, marketing, over-competitive schooling and electronic entertainment.*

(Last paragraph.)

> *As far as I can see, there's a lot more honey than poison in the cocktail that is childhood in the twenty-first century: and my kids, and all the other kids I know, are the sweeter and more promising for it.*

When you see the second paragraph from the passage, the repetition of the image of the 'poisoned cocktail' in the last paragraph helps you to understand how the passage has developed an argument from 'poison' to 'honey', which shows that the 'bad' aspects of childhood are not necessarily the whole story.

Repetition in general, in all its aspects, is an effective structural tool in language. We learn very young the effect of repetition of sound in the form of rhyme and rhythm; and the effect of the repetition of patterns of words in choruses in children's stories; and the effect of the magic of 'three'. The use of repetition in adult writing may be more subtle but it can have powerful effects.

Repetition of sound

Repetition of sound in the form of alliteration is familiar to us as a feature of poetry, but it is also a part of the prose writer's technique.

Example

> *Our children are in danger, fattened on fast food, corrupted by commerce, traumatised by testing. And, at the same time, other children are dangerous, malevolent beneath hooded tops, chaotic in the classroom, perilous on the pavements.*

Here the alliteration in 'fattened on fast food', for example, draws attention to the connection between the *fast* nature of the food and its consequences – *fatness*.

Or take the phrase 'traumatised by testing'. Without the alliteration, 'testing' could be seen as a quite neutral word, but linked by sound to 'traumatised' it makes the experience sound quite terrifying.

Sometimes the clue is in the sound itself. Words such as 'dead', 'doomed' and 'dreaded' contain the drumbeat of a heavy dull sound which adds to the emotional strength of the phrase. On the other hand, 'lighter' sounds such as 'f', 't' and 'l' can express a more frivolous mood, e.g. 'flutter', 'flighty', 'trilling'.

Repetition of words

Example

> *Too much stuff. Endless piles of stuff.*

The repetition of the word 'stuff' emphasises the sheer amount of things and the word choice of 'stuff' suggests in the first place that the things are not particularly valuable or well-chosen – the overall impression is of a pile of useless rubbish.

Repetition of phrases

Example

> *It is a sight at once heartening and shaming. Heartening because it is good to see that people are still willing to give up time, money and effort to care with great sensitivity and respect for those they have never met. Shaming because, in global terms, 'we are a wealthy country', and in a wealthy country people should not go hungry.*

⑦ Question

- How is the phrase 'heartening and shaming' given more force by repetition? (**Answer (20)** on page 88.)

Repetition of structures

Example

> *The worst thing about poverty is a sense of shame. The worst thing about joblessness is a sense of personal dishonour. The sense that you are just a mote in a great pool of floating labour, deprived of choice, will never go away.*

The repetition of the two short sentences, each beginning 'The worst thing about …', makes sure that the reader is focused on just how bad the situation is.

The rule of three

The 'rule of three' or 'triad' describes how using words, phrases, clauses or sentences in groups of three adds power to the ideas. It doesn't really matter what you call this feature of language as long as you explain its effect. There is something very powerful in the use of three terms to catch the attention, to hold interest and to make something memorable.

> ### *Hints & tips* ⭐
>
> *A number of the questions throughout the Analysis section of this book are much narrower and more specific than the questions you may get in the exam. In a typical exam question, you might be asked specifically about word choice or imagery, etc.; but it is equally likely that the question would ask 'by referring to at least two features of language … ' It is on these occasions that you have to remind yourself of the features of language discussed here.*

Famous men throughout the ages have understood and used this:

Julius Caesar:

> *I came. I saw. I conquered.*

It suggests a tremendous sense of power.

Winston Churchill:

> *I have, myself, full confidence that if all do their duty, if nothing is neglected, and if the best arrangements are made, as they are being made, we shall prove ourselves once more able to defend our island home, to ride out the storm of war, and to outlive the menace of tyranny, if necessary for years, if necessary alone.*

Here Churchill uses the trick twice: 'if all …'; 'if nothing …'; 'and if the best …' and, in the second half of the sentence, 'to defend our island home'; 'to ride out the storm'; 'to outlive the menace'.

Barack Obama:

> *If there is anyone out there who still doubts that America is a place where all things are possible; who still wonders if the dream of our founders is alive in our time; who still questions the power of our democracy – tonight is your answer.*

This example is from one of the articles on food banks.

Example

> *It has become normal with astonishing speed. Wages are depressed while bills rise ever upward. Pensions and savings descend to the level of a lottery. Education, once the route to security, has left us with legions of well-read casual labourers. For those not granted even that promise there is the zero hours contract, the bedroom tax, the abolition of any right to social security, and the stigma of poverty.*
>
> *The last of these is nothing new. The poor were always marked out. Now we find elaborate ways to describe the old facts: fuel poverty, food poverty, 'poverty of aspiration'.*

? Question

- Identify two examples where a sequence of three items has been used to create an effect. (**Answer (21)** on page 88.)

Tone

As its name suggests, tone is initially a description of a sound. The tone of a piece of writing becomes obvious when it is read out loud by someone who understands what is going on. You would be in a much better place in the exam if the passages were read out to you in the correct tone – but that is not about to happen!

Hidden tones

It is especially important to catch the tone if the writer is using an ironic, playful, mocking or humorous tone. Unfortunately, if you don't recognise that you are in some way being played with, you could end up misunderstanding what is actually being said.

There is a particularly good example of this trap in one of the passages we looked at on page 48 about the technophobe who didn't use his mobile phone.

Example 1

> I do have a mobile phone, but it's immobile. I never take it out of the house, for fear of triggering some ridiculous trend in which a horde of people march down the street bawling into these sinister little gadgets. If you allowed people to use mobile phones in public, you might end up being forced to listen to them on trains and in cafés, asking noisily whether the invoices have arrived. The prospect is too appalling to contemplate.
>
> …
>
> Nowadays however, protest is most definitely what my email virginity has become. I am living proof that all this frenetic, mostly vacuous, communication is quite superfluous. We all survived without it before it started, and I personally have survived without it ever since. If people really want to contact me they write. If they can't be bothered, or have forgotten how to do it, that's their problem.

The first paragraph only makes sense if you realise that the writer is mocking the actuality of people doing exactly what he is describing, by pretending that it hasn't happened yet and suggesting how appalling it would be if such a situation were to come true. All the words like 'ridiculous', 'horde', 'bawling' and 'sinister' lead up to the idea of 'appalling', but the real clue is in 'If you allowed people to use mobile phones in public' – obviously he knows, and he knows that we know, that this situation already exists, but he is pretending that it doesn't and that the world would be a better place without this phenomenon.

Example 2

> [The sport minister] had recently watched girls aged 7–17 doing inline skating at a YMCA event and said: 'Those girls … looked absolutely gorgeous. They were wearing their socks pulled up – beautiful socks with sequins – and their hair was done; my goodness they could skate.'
>
> Beautiful socks; 'done' hair. I'm swooning as I type, especially on behalf of the seven-year-olds judged on their looks. Never mind, say, Nicola Adams and her gold in boxing at the London

Olympics – where were her sequined socks? Or Gemma Gibbons with her untidy hair and her silver medal in judo. Or Jessica Ennis running about in a really fast and unfeminine manner doing heptathlons.

? Question

- What is the tone of the second paragraph here, and what words or expressions give you evidence for your opinion? (**Answer (22)** on page 89.)

Example 3

They do watch a lot of telly. They spend a fair dollop of time on the computer: sometimes they're genuinely doing their homework! They eat chips. They like chicken nuggets, and burgers. They eat sweets. And what's more, in yet another example of the so-called poison culture in which experts tell us our kids are now being raised, my husband and I spend a fair bit of time actually hoping they'll do well. When they do a test or an exam, we like them to pass it. If they don't come up to scratch we make sure we tell them that they're not doing well enough: you can do better, so do better!

So, presumably, we are nightmare parents, raising a nightmare generation on a poisonous cocktail of junk food, marketing, over-competitive schooling and electronic entertainment.

★ Hints & tips

A number of the questions throughout the Analysis section of this book are much narrower and more specific than the questions you may get in the exam. In a typical exam question, you might be asked specifically about word choice or imagery, etc.; but it is equally likely that the question would ask 'by referring to at least two features of language…' It is on these occasions that you have to remind yourself of the features of language discussed here.

? Question

- What is the overall tone of these two paragraphs?

Answer

- Obviously the parents don't actually think they are 'nightmare parents' – probably the opposite, so you could say that the tone is sarcastic, and that would show that you have recognised that these sentences are not to be taken literally.
- A better description of the tone might be 'sceptical'. The use of 'so-called', 'experts' and 'presumably' cast doubt or scorn on the opinion of the experts about how to bring up children. They, as parents, don't believe the experts.

Straightforward tones

Other tones are easier: anger, indignation, curiosity, nostalgia, enthusiasm, and so on.

Example 1

> *When I do get ground down, when it feels really relentless,*
> *I have to be reminded that this is not for ever and that I'm*
> *travelling emotionally, if not geographically. I'm learning about*
> *myself, developing the patience and sympathy that I never*
> *even thought I lacked. Best of all, Jack and I like each other. I'm*
> *always pleased to see him. We spend nearly every waking hour*
> *together, yet when I'm not with him I miss him. I know what*
> *'poi' and 'sha' mean. Above all, I know in every bone of my body*
> *that I will never regret this. I will not lie on my deathbed and*
> *think, oh, how I wish I'd spent less time with my son.*

? Question

- The tone is probably best described as sincere, enthusiastic or emotional. Consider how you would be able to back up any one of these by using evidence from the paragraph. (**Answer (23)** on page 89.)

Example 2

DIVIDED WE FALL

The poor suffer, the politicians spin … Britain becomes a cruel and nasty place

? Question

- Show how this headline and subheading suggest the tone of the article and the writer's stance on the issue. (**Answer (24)** on page 89.)

Example 3

> *Who truly believes that someone applies to a food bank for fun*
> *or a scam? Who exists a wage slip away from the same oblivion*
> *yet still mutters that folk should be grateful for exploitation*
> *wages?*

? Question

- Identify an appropriate tone in these lines and explain how the evidence supports your choice of tone. (**Answer (25)** on page 89.)

Evaluation of longer extracts and passages

This section is designed to help with two kinds of questions that are typically asked in an exercise dealing with two linked passages – the kind of passages you will face in the exam.

We have had a quick look at some of them earlier in the book, but we need to focus on them a little more closely now because this section is all about **the passage as a whole**.

The two typical questions might be:

- **Evaluate the effectiveness of a paragraph (or possibly of a sentence) as a conclusion to the whole passage (or possibly to a substantial portion of the passage).**
- **Identify key areas on which the two passages agree or disagree (or possibly agree and disagree).**

There are three important skills to help with these questions.

1 identifying the writer's stance or point of view
2 summarising
3 comparing.

Identifying the writer's stance

The writer's stance can be hinted at by **tone**. It also becomes obvious in the course of the article through the **argument** of the passage and the **use of language**. You will notice that many of the examples we have looked at under different language features have been aimed at showing what the writer's **attitude** is to his or her material.

If you read carefully, you should be able to tell what the writer's stance is and to provide evidence to demonstrate why you think so.

Tone

Example 1

All kids want for Christmas is technology

But will those gifts do them more harm than good?

Like many parents, I have been stewing over whether to give the gift of technology to my sons aged six and four. They, of course, like many kids, want their own screens. So why am I reluctant (financial cost aside) to give them what they want?

? Question

- What tone can you identify in this opening to an article on children's use of new media? How does it allow you to infer what the writer's stance is likely to be?

Answer

- The tone is possibly puzzled or ambivalent (remember this word from way back on page 38).
- The writer's stance, therefore, is likely to move from one side of the argument to the other, possibly not reaching any firm decision.

If you wanted to justify your choice of tone you could use the following ideas:

- The use of 'but' shows a contradiction; 'stewing' suggests an inability to decide; the use of self-questioning – 'So why am I … ?'
- The use of an informal register ('kids', 'stewing') and the parenthesis in the last line suggests that the answer will not be an official, expert, formal one.

Example 2

I am not connected

I shall soon be the only EMV (email virgin) left in the country. I have never sent an email, though I've occasionally cheated and asked my teenage son to do so for me. Nor have I ever used the internet. I am no more capable of going online than I am of getting to Saturn. I don't know how to text. I do have a mobile phone, but it's immobile.

Both the headline and the content of this opening show that the tone is light-hearted and mocking, and that the writer's stance is eccentric, deliberately setting his face against modern technology. If you know the term 'Luddite', now would be the time to use it.

Remember

It is really important to check out the tone of the passage and be alert to the fact that there might be irony at work (sometimes coupled with exaggeration) – in which case not all statements can be taken at face value.

Argument

The writer's argument will identify which side the writer is on or it might show that the writer is balanced on the subject and comes down on neither side.

Use of language

All the work in the Analysis section of this chapter helped to identify the writer's stance by taking into account such features as **word choice**, **imagery** and **structure**.

Summarising

This skill of summarising is important in many spheres and not just in the examination. There is a world out there which education is preparing you for. The exam is merely a staging post on the way, not an end in itself – although it may be hard for you to see that as you come closer to taking the exam. In business, ideas have to be summarised, meetings have to be minuted; in any management role, ideas and instructions coming from above in the organisation's structure have to be transmitted in an easily accessible form to the people who will execute them; in medical or legal situations there have to be digests or summaries of consultations; your school reference is a summary of your talents and interests.

In the context of the passages used in the exam, summarising efficiently will help you to understand the whole of the article, or a section of it, rather than merely the little bits you have looked at in the questions.

It is important to be able to summarise quite lengthy passages quickly. This does not mean that you have to write an elegant, short version of what is in front of you. In fact, you don't have to write anything at all. Highlighting might be enough. For our purposes, summarising means being able to notice the important points in the argument of the passage(s) which, eventually, you are going to have to compare. We have already looked at part of this skill on page 34 in Reading paragraphs to **identify argument** and again when discussing **links** on pages 42–46.

The clue to successful summarising lies in understanding how paragraph structure works. You need to be able to:
- identify the topic sentence of a paragraph
- identify any really important development of the topic within the paragraph
- ignore unnecessary detail – examples, lists, descriptions, etc.

Look at the article below, which is about food banks. **Topic sentences** have been underlined for you. **Important developments/ideas** have been highlighted in bold. **Unnecessary detail** includes:
- lines 25–31 – 'The pity … on his own' is an example, not necessary in a summary
- lines 41–49 – 'I spoke to … into care' are again examples.

Example 1

> **Food banks or dignity: is that the choice we offer the hungry?**
>
> The rise of food banks in Britain has been met with shock, and denial. But they cannot cope with a national crisis
>
> *When people used to speak of hunger – as an issue, not a sensation – they used to speak of faraway. Hunger meant the developing world, NGOs, imploring eyes on the TV news. It was, in modern times at least, a distant problem. <u>So it comes as a*
> 5   *shock that in the second decade of the twenty-first century we are speaking about hunger in Britain, right here right now.</u>*

Perhaps we were reassured by the notion that we live in the age of 'relative poverty', when those who were officially deemed poor were not actually destitute but just had less than everyone

10   else. The poor of our era were, we imagined, not Charles Dickens poor. They still had food on the table and a roof over their heads. Perhaps that is why there has been something of a delayed reaction to the rise and rise of genuine hunger in this country. The unkind would call it denial. **But it is becoming**

15   **harder to deny.**

Especially when I visited a Trussell Trust foodbank this week, in Hackney in East London, no more than a three-minute walk from a pleasant green complete with upmarket cafés and a specialist Italian deli. **It is a sight at once heartening and**

20   **shaming.** Heartening because it is good to see that people are still willing to give up time, money and effort to care with great sensitivity and respect for those they have never met. Shaming because, in global terms, 'we are a wealthy country', and in a wealthy country people should not go hungry.

25   The pity of it is inescapable. I saw a man take home a couple of carrier bags filled with the most basic kind of basics: tinned sausages, a can of soup, a packet of pasta. All decent enough, each allocation calculated for balance by nutritionists. Except that you and I would not want to live on that for three days, which is

30   how long it has to last. And the Trussell rules say that he can only get such help twice more. After that, he will be on his own.

Should we be happy that neighbours, not some faceless state bureaucracy, are helping the hungry? Nice in theory, until you see the extreme pressure food banks are under, the days

35   they run out of food, the fact that affluent areas often, and

predictably, get more donations than the poor areas that need most. **That's the trouble with a voluntary system**, designed to give emergency help only: it cannot cope with what is a nationwide crisis.

40   This view of a benign society also fails to reckon with shame. I spoke to a Glasgow volunteer who told me she knows of men too proud to use their local food bank, who instead walk miles out of their way so they can get food for their families without being seen by their neighbours. They cannot afford the bus, and

45   the walk home carrying bags of tins is hard, but it preserves at least some dignity. I learned too of the single mothers who fear visiting a food bank, thereby admitting they cannot feed their children, lest they be deemed incapable and their kids taken into care.

50   This was why Britons sought to put the Victorian era of charity behind us, why we decided that sometimes a state service is better: because there is less shame in claiming a nationally authorised benefit than in going to a church hall, being handed a food parcel and having to nod your head and say thank you.

55   Still, the shame is bearable if the alternative is you or your family going hungry. What has become of us, when that is the choice we offer our fellow citizens: dignity or food? And this in our wealthy, wealthy country.

> ### Hints & tips ⭐
>
> In this exercise not everyone will identify the same topic sentences, nor the same important details. There are no absolutely 'correct' answers; there is a variety of acceptable answers. Whatever form of making notes is most helpful to you is the best. There is no rigid method and no exact formula. Practise on a variety of passages and articles until you find your own preferred method.

❓ Question

- Using the help provided, make some notes to identify the main points/argument of the passage. (**Answer (26)** on page 89.)

The next example is shorter, but it will give you practice in making your own notes on the important ideas. You have seen various parts of this article before, so you have some knowledge of it.

Example 2

All kids want for Christmas is technology

But will those gifts do them more harm than good?

Like many parents, I have been stewing over whether to give the gift of technology to my sons aged six and four. They, of course, like many kids, want their own screens. So why am I reluctant (financial cost aside) to give them what they want?

5   The American Academy of Pediatrics advises that children have less than two hours of screen time a day – and no digital media for the under twos. Yet a survey published last week showed that in the UK around half of two- to three-year-olds – dubbed 'iTods' – are playing on tablets.

10 *So great is the urge to restrict this aspect of children's lives that there are even apps that will switch the machine off when the allotted time is up. Many tech advocates encourage such limits as part of the general boundary-making of parenting.*

15 *Scientific research on the subject is in its infancy and existing research is contradictory. If you believe that 'screen time' is bad for children, you can find a few pieces of research to support that view, which shows correlations with attention defici or with obesity. But there is other research that*
20 *suggests possible benefits: correlations, for instance, between computer skills and better IQs.*

Similarly, where some studies suggest that technology is making us more isolated, there are others that show the opposite. One study found that Facebook users had more
25 *social capital than abstainers, and that the site increased feelings of wellbeing especially in those suffering from low self-esteem.*

And there is a whole tranche of research claiming that technology can be good for children, especially when used in
30 *interaction with real-life scenarios in groups or with parents engaging in play too. This is not technology as babysitter, but as part of the general hard work of coaching and educating. Frankly it sounds a bit of a slog. However, the conclusion appears to be that we should be more relaxed about letting*
35 *children explore technology on their own. The world is changing: we are living in a world of social media and instant access to information. We cannot – and should not – turn the clock back. The problematic aspects of new technologies are also what is really positive about these technologies.*

For a sample summary see **Answer (27)** on page 89.

Hints & tips ★

How you make notes is entirely up to you. No one is going to look at them. They are simply a means to an end – finding the important ideas. You can highlight or even just remember – whatever suits you best.

Summary 👍

1 Identify topic sentences.
2 Identify the main supporting ideas.
3 Cut unnecessary detail.

Comparing

This skill of comparing is necessary to tackle the last question in the exam – the one where you have to compare the two passages.

You will be asked to **identify key** areas on which the writers of the passages **agree** or **disagree** (or possibly, depending on the nature of the passages, where they agree **and** where they disagree). You will also be asked to '**refer in detail** to **both** passages'.

1 Look at the headings of both passages. There will be some information there – a general outline or simply an identification of the topic.
2 Look at the question(s) that ask you to compare the two passages – there will be some clue there as to what you are looking for overall.
3 Read both passages quickly.

Avoid the temptation to get stuck into the questions on the first passage without quickly reading the second one. If you don't read the second one now, you will have no idea where you are ultimately going with the ideas. You will see individual details, but not how these details contribute to the big picture.

When you have read both passages quickly, you can then get down to looking at the questions on Passage 1. Some part of your mind might be worrying away at the second passage even though you are giving your full conscious attention to Passage 1. (This way of working can apply to the Critical Reading paper as well – see page 136.)

When you have finished answering the detailed questions, you should have some idea of the main points and what the writer's stance is.

If there is a question about the conclusion of the first passage, or part of it, might help to give an overview of the important ideas.

Although you may not be asked individual questions on the second passage, you will have to be clear about its main ideas. There is the suggestion at the top of the second passage that 'you may wish' to make notes or to highlight main ideas. Obviously, it is in your own interests to take 'you may wish' and replace it with 'you should' or 'you must'! In the previous section on summarising you have practised doing exactly that. But because you know what you are looking for – agreement – for example, you can possibly skip quite quickly over some areas of Passage 2.

The second part of the question – '**refer in detail** to **both** passages' – means that you have to provide evidence by comment and reference to both passages to substantiate or back up your identification of a key point on which the writers agree (or disagree). So, for each key idea you have to show how that key point is made in **each** passage.

> ## Hints & tips ★
>
> *When you are deciding on which areas are 'key', you have to be selective. There could, in a long passage, be quite a number of agreements, but you are looking to select the most important ones – probably three or four.*

Hints & tips ⭐

You must do what you are asked. If you are asked about 'agree', then you ignore any areas of disagreement; if you are asked about 'disagree', then you ignore any areas of agreement. When you are asked to do both, of course, you do both. You must ignore what your feelings and ideas are on the subject. You are asked to make an objective identification of the main areas of agreement etc., so your views are irrelevant.

The next exercise consists of two passages for comparison:

'I am not connected' (page 50)
'All kids want for Christmas is technology' (pages 77–78)

Read the two passages and answer the question below.

Note: the passages are both much shorter than you would come across in the exam and you have already seen both of them at various points throughout this book.

The value of doing this exercise is not so much in the actual answer, which is very easy, but in the methodology and explanation that follows the answer. Because they are so short, the question only asks for **one** key area of disagreement.

❓ Question

- Both writers express their views about modern advances in communication technology. Identify **one** key area on which they disagree. In your answer you should refer in detail to both passages.

Answer

- The key area of disagreement is whether modern advances in communication technology are good for society or bad.
- The first passage is completely anti-technology/technophobic/ Luddite. He regards all of them as intrusive ('The prospect is too appalling to contemplate') and unnecessary – instead of 'frenetic, mostly vacuous communication', it can be done in old-fashioned writing.
- The second passage, on the whole, comes to the conclusion that these things are good for society. For example, 'Facebook users had more social capital than abstainers' as they increase general happiness and confidence; these means of communication are a valuable part of the world we live in – 'We cannot, and should not, turn the clock back'.

This answer has identified one key area of disagreement and has referred to each of the passages (not all references have to be quotations) to show what each writer's stance is.

Hints & tips ⭐

- *The answer does not refer to parts of the first four paragraphs of the second passage where the writer does have some doubts about the value of the technology, because that would be exploring an area of agreement which is not what you were asked to do.*
- *The answer also does not make any reference to the car accident – that is merely supporting detail, not the key idea.*

The next exercise consists of two passages for comparison, 'To bring girls into sport, get rid of old ideas of femininity' and 'Oh do try to be more feminine, you sporting goddesses'.

Passage 1

To bring girls into sport, get rid of old ideas of femininity

It happened overnight. One minute, I was flying down the wing like a character out of *Bunty*, my only worry in life that I would lose control of the ball and thus let down our captain Caroline 'Caz' Johnson, a girl who seriously demanded to be impressed.

5 The next, I was a *Jackie* photo-strip, obsessed with frosted lipstick and whether my hair looked like Siobhan's out of *Bananarama*.

After this, there was no way back. Reluctant to run or indeed make sudden movements of any kind, I was soon dropped from the hockey team. PE lessons, meanwhile, became a convoluted

10 exercise in avoidance – and not only for me. The slothfulness spread among us girls like a contagion. Cross-country runs began with a truculent jog until we were out of sight of the teachers, at which point we would repair to the nearest newsagent for sweets and a Coke. Rounders involved making sure your team was out as

15 soon as possible, the better that you might field, and get to sun-bathe and gossip in the long grass. Athletics meant hiding in the loos until it was 'too late to change, Miss'.

Needless to say, I never returned to sport, for all that I secretly longed to. At university, I did not row or take up cricket. My 20s

20 were notable for the amount of time I spent sleeping. These days, I run twice a week, but I do it only for my waistline: it's work, and it's lonely work at that.

When my husband comes home from his weekly football game, I am full of envy. The boyish pleasure it gives him! The camaraderie!

25 So when the sports minister said that she worries some women find sport 'unfeminine', I am prepared – unlike some – to give her the benefit of the doubt. Trying for empathy, she missed her ⇒

⇨ footing and ended up sounding only patronising. But, her solution
to the question of why so many women disdain sport – 1.8 million
30 fewer women than men take part in it regularly – certainly sounds
loathsome to me (she considers cheerleading and rollerskating to
be 'very feminine' and thinks those who take part in them look, as
if they were starring in ads for antiperspirant, 'absolutely radiant').

But this doesn't mean that she's wrong about the problem itself. It's
35 the idea of 'femininity' that needs a rethink, not sport. Better still,
we could ditch the word altogether. Meanwhile, we need to stop
thinking of certain other words – 'ambition', 'success', even 'clever'
all come to mind – as dirty when placed in proximity to the name
of a woman. What's wrong with wanting to win, with longing to be
40 good at something? And the lead must come from the top.

Women who have succeeded need to start talking about what they
feel in their guts, however painful they may find this, whatever
damage it may do to the air of diffidence they've spent so many
years carefully cultivating.

45 They need to transmit their excitement, their satisfaction, their
sense of liberation and empowerment.

When I think back to the *Bananarama* days, my hair crisp with
Sun-In and Wella gel, it is this flimsiness that pains me most, the
sense that I would only be noticed, be found attractive, if I was a
50 blonde smile in stretch jeans. I can't deny that in my nylon hockey
skirt and clumpy studded boots, my knees covered in mud and my
sweaty fringe in my eyes, I felt that I looked too substantial, too
challenging. And that feeling stayed with me for years, long after
my hockey stick had been laid to rest in the attic.

55 How I wish I'd known then what I know now, which is that energy,
zest and, above all, strength are twice as attractive as a pampered
skin and at least three times as enduring.

Passage 2

Oh do try to be more feminine, you sporting goddesses

Last Thursday the minister for sport suggested that women who
play sport don't have to feel unfeminine, that sports such as ballet,
gymnastics, cheerleading and even roller-skating, which can be
performed at a high level, can leave those participating looking
5 radiant and very feminine.

She had recently watched girls aged 7–17 doing inline skating at a
YMCA event and said: 'Those girls … looked absolutely gorgeous.
They were wearing their socks pulled up – beautiful socks with
sequins – and their hair was done; my goodness they could skate.'

10 Beautiful socks; 'done' hair. I'm swooning as I type, especially on
behalf of the seven-year-olds judged on their looks. Never mind, ⇨

⇒ say, Nicola Adams and her gold in boxing at the London Olympics – where were her sequined socks? Or Gemma Gibbons with her untidy hair and her silver medal in judo. Or Jessica Ennis running
15 about in a really fast and unfeminine manner doing heptathlons.

Imagine being minister for sport and equalities and thinking that ballet and cheerleading (not actually a sport) are good for the body image of young women.

Cheerleading looks very jolly (I'll give it that much), especially
20 if you spent your formative years watching films and television programmes set in American high schools, most of which make a point of clearly demarcating the pretty and popular cheerleaders from the tragic 'loser' girls who have brains.

Before I wear out my keyboard with dismantling the minister's
25 unfortunate remarks, I should point out that buried inside them is a micro-kernel of truth. At the age of 14 boys don't long to ask you out because you are freakishly strong or because you came to their rescue in a fight, like a roaring teenage she-Hulk.

However, the fact that teenage boys can be intimidated by sporty
30 girls – just as middle-aged men can be cowed by powerful female bosses – is obviously not an ideal state of affairs.

The remedy for such teenage boys does not consist of shunting the problem into sequin-socked sidings. No, the one thing that can gnaw at the dated idea that the only appropriate exercise for girly
35 girls is twerking is the precise opposite – that more girls should do 'proper' sports, and do them free of people labelling them or complaining they lack radiance.

The unfeminine sports are the solution, not the problem.

? Question

- Both writers express their views about girls' sport and femininity. Identify two key areas on which they agree. In your answer you should refer in detail to both passages. (**Answer (28)** on page 90.)

Hints & tips ⭐

- *Some parts of each passage may have nothing to do with the key areas, so you can ignore them.*
- *The tone of each writer is important in showing the writer's stance – especially if that tone has elements of irony, sarcasm or humour.*
- *The evidence in support of each of the key areas should be mixture of quotation/reference and comment. It is not enough just to give a quotation – you have to make a link with your key area.*
- *If you are not asked for a specific number of key areas, you should probably be looking for no more than three or four.*

Summary 👍

1 What **topic** – or **aspect** of the topic – in the passages are you being asked about?
2 Are you being asked about **agreement** or **disagreement** or **both**?
3 **Identify** the **key** areas of agreement or disagreement or both.
4 By referring to **both** passages, provide backing for **each** area you have identified.

Hints & tips ⭐

1 Don't make any reference to your own feelings and attitudes towards the topic.
2 Do check whether the whole topic is to be explored, or an aspect of the topic.
3 Don't identify too many areas of agreement/disagreement – distinguish between the important and the trivial.
4 Don't stray into areas of disagreement if what you have been asked involves areas of agreement – and vice versa.

Answers

There are three important points to make about the answers:

1 These are possible answers – not the only answers.
2 There are many more points contained in these answers than you would need to produce for a given question. Look at the mark allocation and see how many points you will have to make.
3 The **commentaries on the answers** are even more important than the answers themselves because they show the method of arriving at a good answer.

Note: it is not always repeated in every answer but:

1 A reference alone normally gains no marks. A basic comment is worth 1 mark, a well-developed comment can be worth 2 marks.
2 You must use your own words as far as possible: you should make clear you know the meaning of complex words; simple words can obviously be repeated without trying to find a synonym.

Answers

Answer (1) (page 40)

1 The large number and great variety of new forms of communication.

The context of 'proliferation of technology' – the list of items that children now have – helps you to arrive at your answer.

2 The fact that children may be able to outwit their parents or conceal things from them.

The context of 'the challenge to adult authority' – they are more competent than their parents – helps to give you your answer.

Answer (2) (page 41)

1 Participating in clubs sharing your enthusiasms.
2 Volunteering to help in the community.
3 Experiencing the world of business start-ups.

Again, punctuation helps with this answer. There are four sentences in the section of the paragraph you need to use. The last sentence simply gives more details of the charity shop idea. Thus each of the remaining three sentences gives you one point to identify. If you had produced a list of clubs you would be getting tied up in the detail and not seeing the bigger picture in the whole paragraph. You must focus on the 'topics' not the details.

Answer (3) (page 42)

Technology:

- teaches children facts and skills (educational)
- helps children make friends (social)
- helps develop children's imagination through computer games (educational).

Here you have two items in one sentence, and then a longer sentence that you have to work through to see that the main point is that of the development of the imagination. You have been asked about benefits, therefore the mention of violence is not part of your answer.

⇨

Answer (4) (page 43)

The rest of the paragraph offers three main solutions that might help 'employability'. Good exam passes are important, but so are marketable skills such as the ability to work in a variety of situations, creativity and good careers advice, including knowing your personal strengths, making useful choices and researching universities' requirements.

Or it would be acceptable to put your answer in this form:

The rest of the paragraph offers three main solutions that might help to get employment:
- not only good exam passes
- but marketable skills
- and good careers advice.

The development here is in the 'problem/solution' idea: these are solutions to the problem set out in the first sentence. It is then a simple matter to identify these three solutions.

Answer (5) (page 46)

- 'Those demands' are the result of so many people needing to eat fish so more fish needs to be caught, but sustainably.
- 'That', i.e. the need to catch fish sustainably, 'makes it all the more crucial' to stop illegal fishing – which is unsustainable.

Answer (6) (page 48)

The idea of 'the print revolution' and the idea that contradictory research always accompanies new technology are illustrated by the examples of telephone and radio, which are now uncontroversial, and even more spectacularly by the idea that reading novels was once thought to be dangerous for young people.

Answer (7) (page 48)

The anecdote shows that even when a mobile phone could have been legitimately useful (i.e. in an emergency situation), it failed to be of any use. This supports the author's general thesis – that mobile phones are unnecessary/useless.

Answer (8) (page 50)

- The conclusion refers back to the author's description of himself as an email virgin in the opening sentence of the passage.
- The words 'frenetic', with its connotations of lots of useless activity, 'vacuous', with its connotations of emptiness and futility, 'superfluous', with its suggestion of too much useless stuff, all refer to his description of people engaged in banal mobile phone communication.
- The fact that he is not engaged in these forms of communication goes back to the title.
- The last sentence emphasises his stance on the subject by putting all the blame on other people and by making the distinction between important communication and mere remarks, therefore justifying his views (at least to himself).

There is far more in this answer than you would actually be required to write, but it shows understanding of the way in which:
- *writing techniques aid the effectiveness of the ending*
- *the ideas of the passage are summed up.*

Answer (9) (page 53)

- 'sumptuously' suggests the luxury and excessive attractiveness of the fish.
- 'juicy' suggests moist and tasty.

- 'fizzing' suggests something energetic and full of potential.
- 'drizzle of virgin olive oil' suggests a thin stream of something precious added to the fish.
- 'virgin olive oil' suggests fresh, new, unpolluted accompaniment for the fish.
- 'splash' suggests the idea of a chef-like flourish adding to the taste.
- 'zingiest' suggests a fresh and tangy flavour being added to the dish.

Again, there are too many examples here; three would probably be sufficient, but it would depend on the number of marks available. The word 'suggests' is used in these answers to show that you are moving from the reference (for which you get no marks) to the connotative area surrounding the word you have chosen to deal with.

Answer (10) (page 54)

This paragraph does not have so many obvious examples to choose. There are really no words that stand out in the first four lines – all the words are pretty much used in their simple denotational sense.

But the last three lines provide some scope for an answer:
- 'mulling' suggests giving time to thinking over the contents in a leisurely way.
- 'surfing' – although 'surfing the web' is now seen as a simply denotational description of looking up stuff on the internet, 'surfing' still has the feeling of something joyous and exciting.
- 'popping out' suggests the ability to leave the house spontaneously, on a mere whim.
- 'pleasure shopping' suggests shopping not for necessities but for more interesting, must-have items.
- 'shop floor' suggests he is tied to the same place for work and living in a never-ending time loop.

'popping out' and 'pleasure shopping' are the most straightforward. 'mulling' would be good if you knew what it meant. You might not have thought of 'surfing' because you felt it was just (in this context) an 'ordinary' word. And 'shop floor' is a bit more complicated.

Answer (11) (page 55)

The simile 'The slothfulness spread among us girls like a contagion' suggests that slothfulness (laziness) was infectious and began to affect all the girls. Comparing the lack of action to a disease suggests that the writer now thinks this was a bad thing that happened to her and to all the other girls.

Answer (12) (page 56)

By comparing himself and the other househusbands to blue whales, which are solitary creatures who only rarely meet other blue whales but when they do they remain together for a while for companionship, the writer emphasises the fact that there are not very many men in his situation and when they find each other they stick together for mutual support.

Answer (13) (page 58)

'More honey than poison in the cocktail' is seeing life as a drink that the children will take, but the idea that twenty-first century childhood is somehow dangerous (poison) is being opposed by the idea that life is actually very pleasant for these children – as sweet as honey.
Life which the modern child partakes of is made up of good things and bad – this is the literal idea; figuratively, life is seen as a mixed drink (a cocktail) containing good things (honey) and bad things (poison) but with more good than bad.

Answer (14) (page 59)

In this metaphor childhood is seen as a country which is the subject of a dispute, as if people didn't know the boundaries of the country and the geography of the country is like the knowledge of how it feels to be a child in that landscape.

$\Rightarrow$

The metaphor is extended when the country of childhood is forgotten by adults and replaced with their version of the landscape (universe).

You don't need to deal with the extension if you are happy with your answer on the 'territory/geography' idea.

Answer (15) (page 59)

'Plundering shoals' is the obvious metaphor. It suggests that when the ordinary person buys fish in a supermarket, he is acting like a thief or a pirate in 'stealing' from the world's stock of fish, and the stock in the supermarket is described as a 'shoal' because so many of the fish are being sold. This gives the impression that consumption of fish is so great that something needs to be done.

'Zombies' and 'slicing the kitchen knife through the cast of Finding Nemo' *are both possibilities, but much harder to comment on. And there is also a simile: 'shriek like seagulls'.*

You would only be expected to deal with one or two of these. As a guide, look at the number of marks on offer.

Answer (16) (page 59)

The metaphor 'savage' suggests that the fishing system is out of control and violently tearing into the large fish species, just as a dog would savage another animal.

This answer deals with 'savage' as a metaphor; it could also be dealt with as personification. The first part of the answer, up to 'species', would make a perfectly acceptable comment on word choice of 'savage' because it deals with the connotations of savage in this context.

Answer (17) (page 60)

This use of imagery is effective because it suggests that the 'blonde smile' has reduced the girl to a mere aspect of her appearance – ignoring things like the quality of her mind and other worthwhile attributes – which, along with the 'stretch jeans', suggests that she is only interested in her appearance and what effect it will have on others (of the opposite sex).

Answer (18) (page 61)

'Spawned' and 'muscled' are usually used to describe the actions of human beings. Here, 'gastroculture', which is an abstract, is seen to be powerful in creating large numbers of live events and in forcing its way into other larger events which up until now had no need of its services. The words are critical of gastroculture because 'spawned' suggests large quantities of offspring indiscriminately spread around, and 'muscled' suggests the use of physical force to get where it wants to be.

Answer (19) (page 64)

- The semi-colon in the first line defines the two balancing but opposing strands of the argument.
- The list of positive qualities the writer finds in young people – 'imaginative, tenacious, versatile and well-grounded' – suggests that they are well equipped in all areas of personality.
- The short declarative sentence 'If … optimistic' ends the paragraph with a positive climax to the argument.

Answer (20) (page 68)

Each of the two aspects that the writer sees in the food banks is given weight by being repeated at the beginning of the each of the next two sentences, each offering an explanation of what he means by 'heartening and shaming'.

Answer (21) (page 69)

- 'Wages', 'Pensions' and 'Education' begin three successive sentences, each of which presents a pessimistic view of the situation.
- 'fuel poverty', 'food poverty', 'poverty of aspiration' all help to expand the 'stigma of poverty' in the previous paragraph.

$\Rightarrow$

Answer (22) (page 71)

The writer is being sarcastic: she is not 'swooning' in admiration – she regards the comments about 'Beautiful socks' and 'done' hair as totally out of place when talking about sports. The questions are mocking the 'sequined' image which has nothing to do with real women athletes.

Answer (23) (page 72)

- sincere – 'in every bone of my body'; 'I will never regret this'; 'on my deathbed'
- enthusiastic – 'Best of all'; 'always pleased to see him'; 'nearly every waking hour together'; plus some of the ones already mentioned
- emotional – 'travelling emotionally'; 'developing the patience and sympathy'; 'Jack and I like each other'; 'I miss him'; plus some of the ones already mentioned.

Answer (24) (page 72)

- The tone of the article will be serious and probably angry. The words 'suffer' and 'cruel and nasty' are strong negative words that the writer is probably going on to justify.
- The writer's stance is likely to be on the side of the poor and against the politicians.

Answer (25) (page 72)

Tone: angry or indignant.

Quote: the use of questions; 'for fun or a scam'; 'oblivion'; 'exploitation wages'.

Comment:
- The questions have an implied answer, 'No one', which suggests that any right-minded person will agree with the writer's indignation.
- The juxtaposition of 'food bank' with 'fun' and 'scam' suggest that nobody wants to be connected with a food bank.
- 'Oblivion' and 'exploitation' are strongly negative words suggesting that the system is all wrong.

Because you have been asked to 'explain', a simple quotation, while necessary, is not enough. The quotation needs to be connected to a reasonable comment.

You would not use all of these answers. One, well explained, would be enough.

Answer (26) (page 77)

- it is shocking that real hunger exists in twenty-first century Britain.
- poor used to mean deprived of luxuries but not actually hungry.
- but you now see real hunger in food banks.
- good in one way (showing charity)/bad in the other (causing shame).
- charity is fine so long as it works, but sometimes it doesn't.
- charity also causes shame.
- that is why the state took over from charities.
- but if the state no longer provides, food banks are better than nothing.
- but it shouldn't be happening in a wealthy country.

There are lots of different ways of arriving at the main points and noting them. You have to find what suits you.

Answer (27) (page 78)

- problem – is new tech good for kids? (lines 1–4).
- one side says harmful/needs control (lines 5–14).
- research contradictory (lines 15–21).
- isolation possible; but social skills too (lines 22–27).
- good when interactive (lines 28–31).
- conclusion should be relaxed/can't turn the clock back/ on the whole positive (lines 35–39).

⇒

Answer (28) (page 83)

In this question you have been asked to look for two key areas.

One way of starting might be to write down the two key areas you have found.

a) They agree on deploring the minister for sport's view of feminine/unfeminine sports.

OR

They agree that women should be concentrating on qualities other than appearances.

b) They agree that the problem is not the opposition between feminine/unfeminine sports, but with the whole idea of femininity/unfemininity in society.

You could then accumulate the evidence from each of the passages to back up each of these key areas.

Another way is to take each key area in turn and give the relevant supporting evidence, as shown in the following sample answer. You should identify quite clearly where the first of your key areas ends and the next one begins.

a) They agree on deploring the minister for sport's view of feminine/unfeminine sports.

Passage 1 – cheerleading and rollerskating sound 'loathsome' and the writer is sarcastic about the concentration on 'looks absolutely radiant'.

Passage 2 – the concentration on the sequined socks and the 'done hair' are scorned for their pressure on looks and body image.

OR

They agree that women should be concentrating on qualities other than appearances.

Passage 1 – it is not just about sport: women need to embrace words like 'ambition' and 'success', which are thought of as masculine traits.

Passage 2 – the idea is not to stop doing 'unfeminine' sports, but to change people's views on women in general. Unfeminine sports are part of the answer to women's situation.

b) They agree that the problem is not the opposition between feminine/unfeminine sports, but with the whole idea of femininity/unfemininity in society.

Passage 1 – 'It's the idea of "femininity" that needs a rethink, not sport' – the writer thinks the word is unhelpful for enabling women to achieve their deserved position in society.

Passage 2 – the unfeminine sports are the solution, not the problem. The pursuit of real achievement in sport cultivates the strengths needed to take on the world, instead of being obsessed by outward 'attractiveness'.

- *The first four paragraphs of Passage 1 (lines 1–24) can be ignored because the whole issue that the passages have in common is their reaction to the sport minister's statement.*
- *The tone of each passage helps to show the writers' stance(s) – very scathing.*
- *The evidence given in support of each of the key areas is a mixture of quotation/reference and comment.*
- *It is not enough just to give a quotation – you have to make a link with your key area.*
- *The serious point that they are making is that the division between feminine and unfeminine is artificial and unhelpful to women's position in society.*
- *There are two alternatives for the first key area – but whichever one you choose, the idea of body image/appearance has to be there.*

Chapter 4

Reading for Understanding, Analysis and Evaluation Practice Paper

The following two passages focus on the nature of Twitter.

Passage 1

In this passage Ian Bell, writing in the *Sunday Herald*, puts forward his views on Twitter. Read the passage and attempt the questions that follow.

Hints & tips

It would be best not to try this Practice Paper until you are sure you have understood the advice on how to approach the questions.

Is Twitter dumbing us down?

As of this morning, there are 7.2 billion people on the planet.

If you believe every claim, 1.19 billion of them are on Facebook. That's either an awful lot of people wedded to the champion of social media, or an indication of the vastly greater number who can't be
5   bothered or manage without. Ubiquity still eludes the social media.

The best example of this is probably Twitter. Some of its users behave as though all the world is attempting to communicate in messages no longer than 140 characters. The truth can be expressed as pithily: Twitter has a very long way to go before all
10   those grandiose evangelical claims of an interconnected humanity come close to being a reality. As of October 2013, the service had 500 million users – but only 215 million of those were 'active'.

Once I swore I would never have anything to do with Twitter. The number of people capable of saying anything of interest in
15   140 characters struck me as vanishingly small (it is). The number who could resist self-promotion, nastiness, or pursuing politics without using the typographic equivalent of A SHRIEK didn't seem impressive (it isn't). The attractions appeared limited.

Tweeting publicly, you can soon find yourself reminded that
20   the number of people you would cross a street to avoid hasn't diminished since last you checked. When Caroline Criado-Perez was subjected to anonymous threats of rape and death last summer for campaigning to have Jane Austen's image on a banknote, the case against Twitter was pretty convincing. Why
25   volunteer to introduce yourself to scum?

You could make a case. You could say, first, that by avoiding the ugliness and the risks you let thugs win. You could say that the contest about free speech matters. You could argue, above all, that disdain for change is not going to halt change. ⇨

⇨

30 I gave in to Twitter for less elevated reasons: the herd was thundering through. In journalism and politics in Scotland in 2014, a year with some significance, Twitter amounts to an important, if ramshackle, forum. In terms of discourse, it is more like the badlands of the Wild West than Periclean Athens, but as a
35 responsive, collective medium Twitter is as staggeringly fast as it is flawed.

Witnessing the Clutha tragedy as it unfolded was a case in point. That night, journalists and others all over Glasgow and Scotland mounted an impromptu rolling news operation through
40 Twitter that was wondrous to behold. No important fact reached traditional outlets that had not already been sourced and tweeted. A great deal of rubbish and rumour went through the mill, as ever, but the self-organising nature of the thing meant that nonsense was soon weeded out. The story was gathered and told as though
45 by an ideal virtual newsroom.

Twitter is fascinating, meanwhile, if you have any interest in the forms of the written word. A lot of the better tweets are shaped like a classic gag, with set-up and pay-off. A lot of the very worst, even by 'educated' types, simply prove a truism:
50 some people really can't string two sentences together. As for the character limit, I feel an odd nostalgia. If you ever had to write headlines within the unbreakable rules of hot-metal type, when fonts could not by tweaked with clever software, tweeting isn't so hard.

55 But Twitter, like most of the social media, like most forms of digitised communication, attracts all sorts even as it excludes billions. The numbers who think a pinnacle of technological achievement is just a grand excuse for vile and sneaky abuse is staggering – social media bring the witless and the worst flocking,
60 much as dank, cosy shadows attract cockroaches.

And there is an unpalatable fact: clever technology doesn't make the stupid any less stupid. In fact, there are numerous claims that fast, frictionless social media are making things worse – witness the claim from 2008 that attention spans shortened from 12
65 minutes to 5 minutes in the space of a decade.

Is that claim true, however? It might be explained by an impeccable theory (mine): tales of social media reducing attention spans can probably be explained by people failing to pay attention.

Suddenly there was a lot of talk of 'brain plasticity', the loss of
70 the ability to contemplate, of the evaporation of real thinking in an accelerated, overloaded world. Again, however, the scientific evidence was thin. It is too early to tell.

But then, what does anyone need to know? Twitter is utterly facile – how could it be otherwise? If all you know is what
75 Google passes off as the only truth, what can you ever know? If information is grazed and attention flits like a butterfly, knowledge is a glittering shadow.

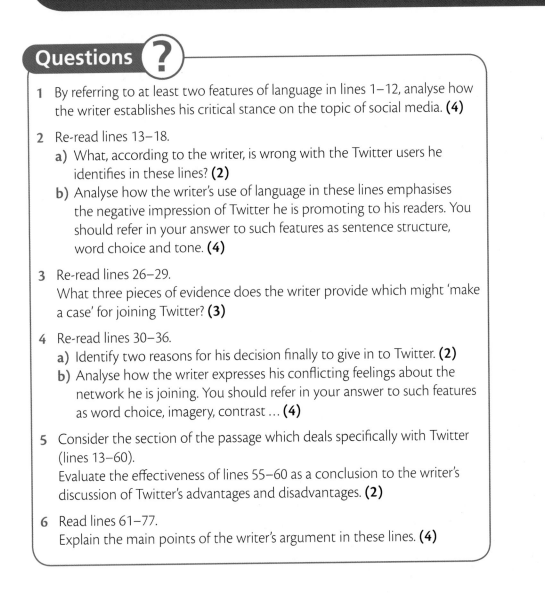

Questions ?

1 By referring to at least two features of language in lines 1–12, analyse how the writer establishes his critical stance on the topic of social media. **(4)**

2 Re-read lines 13–18.
   a) What, according to the writer, is wrong with the Twitter users he identifies in these lines? **(2)**
   b) Analyse how the writer's use of language in these lines emphasises the negative impression of Twitter he is promoting to his readers. You should refer in your answer to such features as sentence structure, word choice and tone. **(4)**

3 Re-read lines 26–29.
   What three pieces of evidence does the writer provide which might 'make a case' for joining Twitter? **(3)**

4 Re-read lines 30–36.
   a) Identify two reasons for his decision finally to give in to Twitter. **(2)**
   b) Analyse how the writer expresses his conflicting feelings about the network he is joining. You should refer in your answer to such features as word choice, imagery, contrast … **(4)**

5 Consider the section of the passage which deals specifically with Twitter (lines 13–60).
   Evaluate the effectiveness of lines 55–60 as a conclusion to the writer's discussion of Twitter's advantages and disadvantages. **(2)**

6 Read lines 61–77.
   Explain the main points of the writer's argument in these lines. **(4)**

Passage 2

In this second passage Josh Constine writes on the website of an organisation called techcrunch.com in November 2013.

Read the passage and attempt the question that follows. While reading, you may wish to make notes on the main ideas and/or highlight key points in the passage.

You should use Twitter because it makes everyone as smart as anyone

Twitter's purpose is still widely misunderstood, and many people think they have no need for it. But it has great potential to enlighten us. Here's how:

We are a specialised species. Each of us lives a different life with
5 unique passions, intellectual pursuits and hobbies. We choose a path and along the way amass a distinct collection knowledge. But what if we could peek into each other's minds to gain insight from the roads we'll never travel? Well, we can. That's the magic of Twitter.

It's inherently flexible. Twitter is a skeleton its users bring to
10 life. Yes, we can share what we're having for breakfast or what we watch on TV. But at its best, Twitter is a tool for distilling understanding of the world into the most digestible format possible.

Imagine a scientist on the other side of the planet. They read
15 and research all day, spending time the rest of us don't have. Then they filter through all the noise and esoteric details, choosing the most important things they've learned. The scientist condenses these complex concepts into simple, widely comprehensible 140-character slices of information, and tweets
20 them. Knowledge.

By following the right people on Twitter, we could see the world like a quantum physicist, movie critic, artist, explorer or entrepreneur. Even 'normal' people have something special to say about how they interpret existence, and there is joy in more
25 vividly seeing our friends' perspectives.

Reading tweets won't make us experts in all these areas. But our mortal lives are short. There's not enough time to grasp the intricacies of everything. Twitter is a shortcut to the next best alternative – understanding through the help of those who truly
30 understand.

But we do need to learn to follow the right people . . . and unfollow the wrong people. Twitter's uncensored stream of information is vulnerable to blatherers more interested in self-promotion and hearing themselves talk than educating their
35 audience. If these challenges can't be beaten, the value of Twitter falls apart.

While humankind has long sought to pool its knowledge, never has the process been so efficient, portable and accessible. We don't have to buy, lug around, and read through hundreds of
40 pages of a book to learn. We needn't lock ourselves in a library or laboratory. And we don't need personal friendships or private meetings with people to hear their thoughts. In fact, Twitter opens a two-way street between us all, ideally creating a conversation, not a broadcast. ⇨

⇨

45   The internet gave everyone a way to share. But Twitter's character
     limit and real-time nature delivers us condensed, pre-filtered,
     ready-to-consume intelligence rather than making us hunt for it.

     Twitter could spawn communities where there were once
     just scattered aficionados who thought they were alone. Its
50   distribution of information could empower the repressed, giving a
     voice to those some sought to silence.

     So if you're asked why Twitter matters, you can tell people that,
     at its heart, Twitter is about leveraging the specialisation of our
     species. So even if we each take a different road, we all reach the
55   destination of wisdom together.

Question ❓

7   Both writers express their views on Twitter. Identify key areas on which
     they disagree. In your answer, you should refer in detail to both passages.

     You may answer this question in continuous prose or in a series of
     developed bullet points. **(5)**

Answers

*These suggestions are not marking instructions. The range of answers which follow offers possible
answers, with advice on the general approach to the task.*

1 Word choice:
   - 'claim' (used twice) suggests that these facts are unsubstantiated.
   - 'can't be bothered' suggests many people show indifference to such things as Facebook.
   - 'manage without' suggests people don't find it at all necessary.
   - 'still eludes' suggests that universal coverage slips away and can't be grasped.
   - 'behave as though all the world' – 'as though' casts doubt on the truth of the
     statement that 'all the world' is involved.
   - 'grandiose' – exaggerated.
   - 'evangelical' – zeal to spread the word over the whole human world.

   Sentence structure:
   - The declarative (or summative) short sentence 'Ubiquity still eludes the social media' suggests
     the writer's confidence in this statement that the social media have not succeeded. (You may
     not know what 'ubiquity' means, although the context might help you to work it out; but that
     need not stop you from noticing the short sentence and its probable function.)
   - The use of the colon in line 9 – 'as pithily:' introduces an expansion of the idea which makes
     clear in an economical way that the writer thinks Twitter's claims are still very far from being true.
   - The inverted commas round 'active' could possibly seem as casting some sort of criticism of
     the practice itself, as if writing 140 character messages were lazy and inactive.

   Another possibility:
   - The use of statistics to prove his point certainly seem to be conclusive – only 215 million out
     of a world population of 7.2 billion, which is a tiny percentage (0.029% actually, not that you
     would be expected to work that out – it's not an arithmetic paper you are sitting!).

⇨

You have been asked to consider at least two features, so an answer that depended entirely on word choice (for example) could not gain full marks.

Remember that if you simply quote the word or phrase (such as 'grandiose') or simply identify a feature (such as 'use of colon') without making a sensible comment on its effect, you will gain no marks. Any four of these 11 points with a sensible comment should gain you at least one mark each – possibly more if the point is well developed.

There may well be other features such as tone or paragraphing – the single sentence opening paragraph – and so on: there is no list of features, and so you are free to deal with any language feature you can identify.

2 **a)** ● Only a very few people have the ability to say anything meaningful in 140 letters, so it's not worth reading most of the messages.
   ● Lots of people use it only to boast about themselves/to abuse others/to promote dodgy political ideas.

These answers have been careful to use their own words but when it comes to something like 'politics' used in this sequence, there is little point in trying to translate it into something less precise like 'sociological, democratic processes' … life is too short!

b) Sentence structure:
   ● Parallel structure of the two sentences beginning 'The number' allows you to appreciate that tiny size of the 'good' as against the massive number of the 'bad'.
   ● The two uses of parenthesis (it is) and (it isn't) again allows you to make the contrast between the two types.
   ● The short first sentence is a dismissive summing up of his reasons for avoiding Twitter.
   ● The short last sentence is also dismissive – it is obvious to the writer that Twitter is of little interest.

Word choice:
   ● 'vanishingly small' suggests that the number of those who would be worth communicating with is so small that it becomes difficult even to see them as they disappear into the distance.
   ● 'self-promotion' suggests bombastic people are best avoided.
   ● 'nastiness' suggests spite – a desire to make someone uncomfortable.

Imagery:
   ● 'the typographic equivalent of A SHRIEK' suggests that the use of things like capital letters to emphasise that these tweets just ends up sounding as if the letters themselves are literally 'shouting' at you.

Tone:
   ● is dismissive/superior – he thinks his opinion is better. This is shown by such things as '(it is)', '(it isn't)'.

Typography:
   ● 'A SHRIEK' is a typographic device to demonstrate what he is talking about – over-emphasis.

Any of these ten points with a sensible comment should gain you at least one mark each – possibly more if the point is well developed.

But remember that if you simply quote the word or phrase (such as 'nastiness') or simply identify a feature (such as 'use of parenthesis') without making a sensible comment on its effect, you will gain no marks.

In this question there is a list of suggested features to help you with your answer by reminding you of them – and it is pretty certain that you will find examples of these features. It is, however, an open list and so you are free to notice other features such as the typography.

3 • to avoid letting the bullies go unchallenged.
   • to uphold the idea that people should be free to speak their minds.
   • because it is not going to go away/ignoring the new world of digital communication won't stop it.

These three points would gain three marks. Note that in this kind of question you have to remember the assumption that you have to 'use your own words'.

4 **a)** • He feels he is being left behind because everyone else belongs to Twitter.
   • 2014 is going to be important to journalists so he doesn't want to miss things.
   • Twitter is a place where discussion will happen.

Any two of these for two marks.

b) Word choice:

• 'less elevated reasons' suggests that he was almost ashamed of his giving in to the pressure.
• 'ramshackle' suggests that although active, the structure is likely to topple over.
• 'the badlands of the Wild West' suggests that the debate it is a free-for-all without any rules.
• 'Periclean Athens' suggests the civilised debates in ancient Athens in a very controlled and structured environment.
• 'staggeringly fast' suggests that one of the virtues of Twitter is that word spreads unbelievably quickly – possibly before waiting for verification.
• 'flawed' suggests that everything is not always true.

Imagery:

• 'herd thundering through' suggests that the rush to join Twitter is as mindless as cattle stampeding, and just as unstoppable, but that he is being carried along by it almost against his will.

Contrast:

• Contrast between the Wild West and Ancient Athens shows the two contrary sides of Twitter.
• Contrast between 'fast' and 'flawed' shows the good and the bad.

Sentence structure:

• The use of the colon in line 30 'less elevated reasons:' introduces the reason – everyone else was already there. It shows the pressure he felt to conform.

You have been given no specific number of features and the list of features is 'open', so you are free to make comment on any aspect of language you notice.

But, you are asked to deal with his 'conflicting feelings', so there must be at least one reference and comment on each side of the conflict – his 'good' feelings and his 'bad' feelings.

One of the suggested features is 'contrast': this is meant to be a helpful suggestion to remind you of the need to look at both sides.

Any four of these ten points with a sensible comment should gain you at least one mark each – possibly more if the point is well developed, so long as at least one reference is made to each side. But remember that if you simply quote the word or phrase (such as 'ramshackle') or simply identify a feature (such as 'use of contrast') without making a sensible comment on its effect, you will gain no marks.

⇨

5 • The writer concludes his discussion of Twitter by returning to one of his initial points – that it is a forum for some rather unpleasant people – 'nastiness' and 'threats of rape and death'. He states in the same paragraph that the number of people of bad intent is 'staggering' in volume.

• Although he does mention some advantages of Twitter in lines 26–45, he returns to his original criticisms in lines 55–60 which makes an effective ending to his argument about Twitter, by leaving the reader with an unpleasant impression of it.

• The use of pejorative words/phrases/imagery is brought to a climax by the language of the last sentence: 'the witless and the worst flocking, much as dank, cosy shadows attract cockroaches'. The simile comparing some Twitter users to 'cockroaches' suggests really unpleasant people, thriving in unwholesome darkness, creating mould and deterioration.

• This recalls his descriptions earlier on of 'scum' suggesting the filthy surface of stagnant water, and 'thugs' suggesting an unintelligent use of brute strength to destroy other people.

This answer includes both ideas and language features, and is more detailed than would be necessary. Any of these attempts or any combination of the individual points would gain two marks.

6 • New digital technology has been blamed for reducing the time that people appear to be able to concentrate for.

• His theory, on the contrary, is that people just don't pay much attention to what they read and hear anyway.

• But possibly the whole pace and bombardment of information is too much for our brains – although this theory has not been proved.

• But, finally, the kind of knowledge gained in this way is ultimately too superficial to be of much use.

It is likely that each of these four paragraphs will provide you with a 'topic' point. 'Explain' implies making some sort of connection – 'on the contrary', 'but', 'but finally'. Remember to use your own words throughout.

7 • There is no need to set out your answer in a table like the one below. It is laid out here to clarify the ideas in these particular passages. You should find your own way of answering this question. Look at the foot of the table for further advice.

⇨

⇨

Areas of disagreement		
	Passage 1	Passage 2
1 Quantity of knowledge	Very few have anything useful to pass on – vanishingly small.	Increases our knowledge/potential to enlighten us.
2 Quality of knowledge	The type of knowledge passed on by Twitter is essentially shallow/dumbing down – self-promotion, nastiness, pursuing political points.	Tool for distilling the understanding in the most digestible form.
3 Attitude to others	Twitter increases our ability to abuse each other – anonymous threats.	Sharing of information is a joy – something special to say.
4 Promoting communication	Twitter gives a voice to the pompous and nasty – people you would cross the street to avoid.	Twitter gives an empowering voice to the repressed/spawns communities who lend members mutual support.
5 Facts versus wisdom	Twitter knowledge is not worth having – information is grazed/attention flits like a butterfly.	Allows us to reach the destination of wisdom/hastening the specialisation of our species.

There is some area of overlap among these points – 2 and 5 are quite similar, but 2 is dealing with the inherent worth or quality of the knowledge whereas 5 is dealing with each writer's conclusion about the worth of the knowledge to the human race.

In this kind of question you may be asked to look for a specific number of points but, if not, you should probably be looking for three or four key areas.

One way of starting might be to write down the three or four key areas you have found. You could then accumulate the evidence from each of the passages to back up each of these key areas. Or you might take each key area in turn and give the relevant supporting evidence.

You can use bullet points or you can write a short paragraph to set out your evidence.

It is helpful to identify quite clearly where the first of your key points ends and the next one begins. It helps you to keep your ideas in order and perhaps prevents you from making the same point twice.

Chapter 5

Critical Reading

This is the second exam paper that you have to sit in your external exam. You have 1 hour and 30 minutes to complete two tasks:

Section 1: 20 marks

Read an extract from a Scottish text or a Scottish poem (or an extract from a Scottish poem) from the list specified and attempt the questions.

Section 2: 20 marks

Write one critical essay on a previously studied text from Drama, Prose, Poetry, Film and TV Drama or Language Study.

There are two other restrictions on what you can and can't do.
1 You must not use the same **text** twice.
2 Each of your answers must be on a different **genre**.

For example, if you have answered on Scottish poetry in Section 1, you cannot write your critical essay on poetry of any kind, Scottish or English.

How you approach your choice will depend on which texts you have been taught and which you have prepared for the exam. For example:
1 You might have been taught three or more specified Scottish texts in different genres taken from the specified list.
2 You might have been taught two specified Scottish texts and one or more texts from outside the list, each in a different genre.
3 You might have been taught one specified Scottish text and one or more texts from outside the list, in different genres.

If you have prepared two or three specified Scottish texts then you obviously should look at both Section 1 and Section 2 questions before you make your choice, but even if you have only studied one Scottish text – and therefore have no choice in Section 1 – you might like to look at the following advice.

There is some psychological evidence to suggest that if you very quickly scan the questions in Section 2 before getting down to answering Section 1, then some part of your brain can work away at clarifying your choice for Section 2 while the 'active' part of your brain is actually busy answering the questions in Section 1. You might like to try this to see if it works for you.

Section 1 is where your choice of text is limited to the list of Scottish texts. You must answer on **one** of the 14 texts presented to you in the paper.

Your choice of text in Section 1 limits your choice of **genre** in Section 2.

The best way to illustrate this, rather than dealing in abstract 'ifs', is to look at aspects of Critical Essay choices (see pages 149–52) once you have clearly understood the requirements for Section 1.

Section 1: Scottish text

There are two important pieces of advice that apply to all the following examples of Scottish text questions:

1 Lots of the work you have done on Understanding, Analysis and Evaluation in Chapter 4 of this book is applicable to the questions on the Scottish text you choose for Section 1.

2 The list of features mentioned in the boxes that precede each of the genres in Section 2 of the exam paper will remind you of the kind of things you may wish to consider when answering the questions in Section 1.

In an English course, nothing is wasted. All the skills are transferrable!

Hints & tips ⭐

If you haven't already done so, read the Introduction at the start of this book, because it gives you useful advice on how to use this book effectively.

Poetry

Poetry is probably the best genre to start with as (most of) the texts are short and self-contained, so that we can look at a complete example.

You might think also that poetry is easier than prose or drama because the texts are shorter – the six poems listed for Norman MacCaig amount to only 158 lines, for example. But you have to know these poems so well that you can quote readily from all of them. You will have one poem in front of you in the paper, for which you can gain the first 10 marks. The next 4 marks bridge the gap between this poem and another you must refer to. The last 6 marks are available for your ability to refer in detail to at least one other suitable poem by MacCaig.

There are **two** possible types of poetry texts you may be asked to deal with here. The first is a **complete poem**, e.g. 'Originally' by Carol Ann Duffy (see below), and the second **an extract from a longer poem**, e.g. from 'Mrs Midas' by Carol Ann Duffy (pages 106–107).

There are also **two** kinds of final 10-mark questions:

1 One kind is concerned with identifying a common **theme or central concern**.

2 The second kind is concerned with the use of a **similar technique or set of techniques**. This type of question appears in the exercise on 'Anne Hathaway' by Carol Ann Duffy (page 109).

Poetry A: a complete poem

Originally

We came from our own country in a red room

which fell through the fields, our mother singing

our father's name to the turn of the wheels.

My brothers cried, one of them bawling, *Home,*

5   *Home,* as the miles rushed back to the city, ⇨

⇨ the street, the house, the vacant rooms

where we didn't live any more. I stared

at the eyes of a blind toy, holding its paw.

All childhood is an emigration. Some are slow,

10 leaving you standing, resigned, up an avenue

where no one you know stays. Others are sudden.

Your accent wrong. Corners, which seem familiar,

leading to unimagined pebble-dashed estates, big boys

eating worms and shouting words you don't understand.

15 My parents' anxiety stirred like a loose tooth

in my head. *I want our own country*, I said.

But then you forget, or don't recall, or change,

and, seeing your brother swallow a slug, feel only

a skelf of shame. I remember my tongue

20 shedding its skin like a snake, my voice

in the classroom sounding just like the rest. Do I only think

I lost a river, culture, speech, sense of first space

and the right place? Now, *Where do you come from?*

strangers ask. *Originally?* And I hesitate.

Carol Ann Duffy

Questions ?

1 By referring closely to verse 1 (lines 1–8), analyse the use of poetic technique to describe the feelings of the persona/poet. **(2)**

2 Analyse the use of poetic techniques that help to convey the anxieties hinted at in verse 2 (lines 9–17). **(4)**

3 How do the ideas of the last section of the poem from 'Do I only …' to the end (lines 21–24) justify the choice of 'Originally' as the title of the poem? **(4)**

4 By referring to this poem and at least one other by Carol Ann Duffy, show how the idea of the outsider is explored in her poetry. **(10)**

Hints & tips ★

*If you have a choice between this Scottish text and another, you should look carefully at **all** the questions asked on **this poem**. You may be quite happy with the choice of 'Originally' because it is a poem you know well and have enjoyed. Questions 1, 2 and 3 may be fine, but question 4 — which is worth 10 marks — asks about the idea of 'the outsider'. The problem is deciding which other poem or poems by Carol Ann Duffy explore this theme — and do you know them well enough to find relevant references for your answer? You should **always** have looked at Section 2 before making your choice.*

Answer

This section takes you through a set of possible answers. Remember though that there will be many other, equally acceptable, answers.

1 **By referring closely to verse 1, analyse the use of poetic technique to describe the feelings of the persona/poet. (2)** ⇨

⇨
There are several possibilities:
- word choice: 'own country'
- imagery: 'fell through the fields'
- imagery: 'the miles rushed back'
- climax/anti-climax: 'the city, the street, the house, the vacant rooms'
- word choice: 'vacant rooms'
- word choice: 'stared' or 'blind toy' or 'holding its paw'.

Exercise 1

Take each of the suggested references in this list (except 'vacant rooms') and provide a relevant comment on each, linking it to the poet's feelings.

(Answers on page 131.)

It would be difficult to use evidence from lines 3 and 4 because they are about the parents and the brothers, not the poet.

It is better to be as specific as you can in your answer. If you choose word choice, you might look at the connotations of two of the words mentioned above. If imagery, you could look in close detail at one or two of the images. Climax has only one example but a satisfactory explanation of how it worked would provide a good answer.

Look at the allocation of marks. There are 2 marks for this question, so it would be foolish to mention every technique you identify. Two good examples should gain the 2 marks.

Avoid taking a long blanket quotation, covering a lot of the words, and making a generalised comment about technique without specifying exactly what you are talking about.

For example:
- **Reference:** 'I stared/at the eyes of a blind toy, holding its paw.'
- **Comment:** The word choice makes you feel that the poet is sad, and needs to be comforted.

The weakness of this answer is that it is too generalised to gain any credit. The comment is true but no specific analysis has been done.

Hints & tips ⭐

*Remember, as in the Reading for Understanding, Analysis and Evaluation Paper, it is not enough to identify the words, phrases, technique or feature you have chosen; you must show **how** these words, phrases or techniques are effective in showing us the poet's feelings. There is no mark for simple identification.*

For example, if you say that the word choice of 'vacant rooms' is effective, and nothing more, you have not really analysed the phrase. You would have to comment on the connotations of 'vacant', which suggests an emptiness, a lack of the people who once lived there – a sort of abandonment. This shows the poet's feelings of loss and regret.

Exercise 2 🖉

Take each of the suggested references in the list of bullet points in the answer to question 2 below (except the loose tooth image) and provide a relevant comment on each, linking it to 'anxieties'.

(Answers on page 131.)

Answers

2 **Analyse the use of poetic techniques that help to convey the anxieties hinted at in verse 2. (4)**
The most obvious choices here are imagery and word choice:
- Imagery: 'All childhood is an emigration', 'anxiety stirred like a loose tooth in my head'.
- Word choice: 'resigned', 'unimagined', 'big boys eating worms', 'don't understand' (these are the most obvious ones, but other possibilities exist).

You could also talk about:
- Contrast: 'some are slow'/'others are sudden'.
- The use of direct speech.

You are being offered 4 marks for this question, so it is safer to deal with at least two techniques in detail. Alternatively, you could give four examples of the same or different techniques with less detail. Remember that simply identifying the image is not enough. There has to be a comment on its effectiveness in exploring 'anxieties'.

For example:

'anxiety stirred like a loose tooth in my head' uses a simile to suggest the constant nagging of the worries the poet has and her inability to forget them, in the same way that your tongue keeps finding out and disturbing a loose tooth.

3 **How do the ideas of the last section of the poem from 'Do I only ...' to the end (lines 21–24) justify the choice of 'Originally' as the title of the poem? (4)**
This question is really about the effectiveness of a conclusion – a concept you have already looked at in Reading for Understanding, Analysis and Evaluation on pages 48–50.

You must link the ideas in these lines with the idea of 'Originally'. The most obvious tie-up is that 'Originally?' is used as a question in the last line, showing that the poem has been an illustration of how hard a question that is to answer. The ideas of 'first space' refer back to the first verse with its references to vacant rooms, and the city, street and house that Duffy left as a child. The question as to whether she really has lost her cultural roots is now not clear to her – 'Do I only think …?' shows the doubt. Therefore, the answer to the question as to where she comes from 'originally' is now obscured by time – 'then you forget, or don't recall' such things as changing her accent and blending into her new background.

4 **By referring to this poem and at least one other by Carol Ann Duffy, show how the idea of the outsider is explored in her poetry. (10)**
*To make sure you answer all the parts of this last question you must do **three** things:*
A *You should show how your understanding of the idea of 'the outsider' has been developed.*
B *Next you should show how the idea of 'the outsider' has been dealt with in the text in front of you.*
C *For the 6 additional marks available you need to refer to the idea of 'the outsider' in one (or more than one) of the other poems by Carol Ann Duffy you have studied. In this case 'War Photographer' could provide the material you need.*

For example:
A An outsider can be seen as someone who is divorced from their roots and finds it difficult to relate to a new set of customs and values. This feeling of isolation and dislocation marks the

⇨

outsider in other sets of circumstances where the values of the society differ from his or her own.

B 'Originally' is about being uprooted from her place of birth and her distress as a child needing the comfort of 'holding its paw'. There is a lack of a sense of identity in the last two lines – 'And I hesitate'.

Parts A and B could be dealt with together, but the general idea of 'the outsider' and the particular application of that idea to this poem would both have to be covered.

C *You would be expected to make references to the other poem you have chosen to look at – in this case, 'War Photographer' – showing how each of them backs up the idea that the persona of the poem is an outsider.*
   - *'He has a job to do'/'to do what someone must'*
   - *'A hundred agonies'/'pick out five or six'*
   - *'between bath and pre-lunch beers'*
   - *'he earns a living and they do not care'.*

You can answer this question either by the use of bullet points or in a series of linked statements. Both of these methods are shown below.

Bullet points

- 'He has a job to do'/'to do what someone must' shows that he is somehow set outside society and is doing a job that others would not be keen on doing because of having to witness the pain.
- 'A hundred agonies/pick out five or six' suggests that the society he comes back to with his hundred photographs will only be shown a selection – a selection that has just been 'picked out' seemingly at random and not chosen carefully. Society will never know the full force of the horror he has witnessed – 'how the blood stained into foreign dust'.
- 'between bath and the pre-lunch beers' – society is affected by his photographs only temporarily; he is different – the knowledge is permanent.
- 'he earns a living and they do not care' ends the poem showing definitely his isolation from the rest.

Series of linked statements

In 'War Photographer', the photographer's job sets him apart from the rest of society. He is 'alone' and 'has a job to do', which is to communicate the suffering he has witnessed in war zones – 'how the blood stained into foreign dust'. The developing photographs remind him of the horrors he has seen and how he 'must' show the violence so that people at home will be moved to think about foreign wars and atrocities. But his isolation from the society that surrounds him is emphasised by the fact that, on the whole, society does not want to know. In fact, only a tiny selection of his work will be allowed to have an effect – his 'editor will pick out five or six'. The fact that 'pick out' is used instead of 'choose' shows that even the selection is slightly random, not carefully thought through. The photographs only have a temporary effect on the readers whose 'eyeballs prick with tears between bath and pre-lunch beers', whereas the effect on him is more lasting – as a result he has to steel himself against the emotion – 'stares impassively'. The last line – 'he earns a living and they do not care' – shows finally what the gulf is between him and the rest of society and how he is isolated because of what he has seen, but which he can only communicate in part.

Two important ideas well explained (with references) or three of them explained in a simpler way would support an answer to the question. But it is not an easy task. You have to select relevant references and link them with the idea of 'the outsider'.

> ⇨
>
> *There is a lot to remember in poetry answers such as these, but you have had the advantage of tackling these poems in detail in class, so you should know them in well enough to make relevant and accurate references to them in your responses to this kind of question.*
>
> *Other poems from the selection could also be used:*
>
> - *'Havisham' explores Miss Havisham's position as an outsider from the world of men which has treated her so badly.*
> - *'Mrs Midas' deals with her relationship with her husband who becomes an outsider as a result of his foolish (she says selfish) wish which has destroyed their intimacy.*
>
> *The only poem of the selection that would be completely inappropriate is 'Anne Hathaway'.*

Hints & tips ★

*If you have a choice between this Scottish text and another, you should look carefully at **all** the questions asked on **this poem**. You may be quite happy with the choice of 'Mrs Midas', but always look at the **last** question (in this case, question 4) to see how easily it allows you to show your knowledge of the selection of poems you have read. Before you make up your mind finally, you should **always** have looked at Section 2 before making your choice.*

Poetry B: an extract from a longer poem

Mrs Midas

It was late September. I'd just poured a glass of wine, begun

to unwind, while the vegetables cooked. The kitchen

filled with the smell of itself, relaxed, its steamy breath

gently blanching the windows. So I opened one,

5   then with my fingers wiped the other's glass like a brow.

He was standing under the pear tree snapping a twig.

Now the garden was long and the visibility poor, the way

the dark of the ground seems to drink the light of the sky,

but that twig in his hand was gold. And then he plucked

10 a pear from a branch – we grew Fondante d'Automne –

and it sat in his palm, like a lightbulb. On.

I thought to myself, Is he putting fairy lights in the tree?

He came into the house. The doorknobs gleamed.

He drew the blinds. You know the mind; I thought of   ⇨

⇨

15 the Field of the Cloth of Gold and of Miss Macready.

He sat in that chair like a king on a burnished throne.

The look on his face was strange, wild, vain. I said,

What in the name of God is going on? He started to laugh.

I served up the meal. For starters, corn on the cob.

20 Within seconds he was spitting out the teeth of the rich.

He toyed with his spoon, then mine, then with the knives, the forks.

He asked where was the wine. I poured with a shaking hand,

a fragrant, bone-dry white from Italy, then watched

as he picked up the glass, goblet, golden chalice, drank.

25 It was then that I started to scream.

Carol Ann Duffy

Questions ?

1 Referring to at least two examples, analyse the use of poetic technique to create mood in verse 1. **(2)**

2 In what ways is the language of verse 4 effective in building up to the climax 'It was then that I started to scream'? **(4)**

3 Identify and analyse aspects of the language or structure in this extract which create a believable narrative voice for the persona. **(4)**

4 By referring to this poem and at least one other by Carol Ann Duffy, show how effectively she explores the joys and sorrows of a close relationship. **(10)**

Exercise 3 ✎

Attempt to answer questions 1, 2 and 3. Even if you have not studied Carol Ann Duffy's poetry as a specified text, answering these three questions should not be too difficult as the text is there in front of you.

(Answers on page 132.)

This section takes you through a possible answer to question 4. Remember, though, that there will be many other equally acceptable answers.

4   **By referring to this poem and at least one other by Carol Ann Duffy, show how effectively she explores the joys and sorrows of a close relationship. (10)**

*To make sure you answer all the parts of this last question you must do **three** things:*

A   *You should show how your understanding of the joys and sorrows of a close relationship have been developed.*

B   *Next you should show how the idea of the close relationship has been dealt with in the text in front of you.*

C   *For the 6 additional marks available you need to refer to the idea of the joys and sorrows of a close relationship in one (or more than one) of the other poems by Carol Ann Duffy you have studied. In this case 'Valentine' could provide the material needed.*

For example:

A   The joys and sorrows of a relationship are ever-present and can tip quickly from one state to the other – from deep happiness to its reverse – with a sense of mourning for a lost relationship.

B   In 'Mrs Midas' the warmth of the kitchen, the relaxation and anticipation of a happy, contented evening – 'begun to unwind' – is destroyed. 'I miss most, even now, his hands, his warm hands on my skin, his touch' effectively shows how sad she is that their physical relationship can no longer exist, although in the past 'we were passionate then' – their relationship was good. 'separate beds' is symbolic too.

Parts A and B could be dealt with together, but the general idea of the joys and sorrows involved in a close relationship and the particular application of that idea to this poem would both have to be covered.

C   *You would be expected to make references to the other poem you have chosen to look at – in this case, 'Valentine' – showing the idea of the joys and sorrows of a close relationship. You can answer this question either by the use of bullet points or in a series of linked statements. Both of these methods are shown below.*

Bullet points

- 'Not a red rose or a satin heart/I give you an onion' seems to show two opposites – a red rose is usually symbolic of love and an onion is known to give rise to tears.
- 'Not a cute card or a kissogram/I give you an onion' goes further and suggests that the usual Valentine stuff is worthless and that the onion symbolises something more sincere, but which can cause deep emotion – not all the feelings are joyful, though.
- 'Possessive and faithful' sounds quite optimistic, but it is followed by 'for as long as we are', which suggests that maybe it is not permanent.
- The last lines seem to say that a wedding ring can be lethal, connected with the onion scent on the knife used to cut it into rings – a wedding ring.
- The overall impression of the poem is that love can be strong and violent, 'fierce kiss', but also tender and soft, 'light/like the careful undressing of love'.

Series of linked statements

In 'Mrs Midas', the sorrows of having lost an intimate relationship are effectively illustrated several times in the rest of the poem. Obviously she has to avoid being touched by him – 'separate beds' are symbolic of this – but the fact that 'we were passionate then' (in the past) makes it worse. Although we can see from the word choice she is in some way attracted by the beauty of the gold – the 'beautiful lemon mistake' of the hare which he has touched – she has to accept that

⇨

⇒

she had 'married the fool'. However, the poem ends almost tragically after she has severed all contact with him, with the sorrowful lines 'I miss most,/even now, his hands, his warm hands on my skin, his touch.'

In 'Valentine', there is the same sorrow, not of a lost love, but of a love that might be lost in the future – a troubled love.

The 'red rose' and 'satin heart' are ignored in favour of an onion, which first promises the joys of a loving relationship – 'It promises light/like the careful undressing of love'. The onion seems to become next a symbol of truth, even though the truth can be painful 'a wobbling photo of grief'. The 'cute card or a kissogram' are seen to be trivial, not representing the strong passion they have; 'fierce kiss will stay on your lips', but then the ambivalence becomes apparent again – 'possessive' sounds more damaging than 'faithful' and 'for as long as we are' could signal the end of the affair. The last lines seem to say that a wedding ring can be lethal, connected with the onion scent on the knife used to cut it into rings – a wedding ring.

The overall impression of the poem is that love can be strong and violent ('fierce kiss'), but also tender and soft ('light/like the careful undressing of love').

Two important ideas well explained (with references) or three of them explained in a simpler way would support an answer to the question. But it is not an easy task. You have to select relevant references and link them with the idea of joys and sorrows of a close relationship.

There is a lot to remember in poetry answers such as these, but you have had the advantage of tackling these poems in detail in class, so you should know them in well enough to make relevant and accurate references to them in your responses to this kind of question.

There are several poems within the specified list that would suit the question, and many other of Carol Ann Duffy's poems (especially those from the collection entitled Rapture.*) The difficulty is perhaps reminding yourself how a close relationship is portrayed in the rest of 'Mrs Midas'.*

Poetry C

Anne Hathaway

The bed we loved in was a spinning world

of forests, castles, torchlight, clifftops, seas

where we would dive for pearls. My lover's words

were shooting stars which fell to earth as kisses

5 on these lips; my body now a softer rhyme

to his, now echo, assonance; his touch

a verb dancing in the centre of a noun.

Some nights, I dreamed he'd written me, the bed

a page beneath his writer's hands. Romance

10 and drama played by touch, by scent, by taste.

In the other bed, the best, our guests dozed on,

dribbling their prose. My living laughing love –

I hold him in the casket of my widow's head

as he held me upon that next best bed.

Carol Ann Duffy

Hints & tips ⭐

*If you have a choice between this Scottish text and another, you should look carefully at **all** the questions asked on **this poem**. You may be quite happy with the choice of 'Anne Hathaway', but always look at the **last** question (in this case, question 4) to see how easily it allows you to show your knowledge of the selection of poems you have read. Before you make up your mind finally, you should **always** have looked at Section 2 before making your choice.*

1. By referring to lines 1–3, analyse the language the poet uses to create a sense of delight. **(4)**
2. Referring to at least two examples from lines 3–7 ('My lover's words … noun'), analyse the use of imagery to convey aspects of the persona's relationship with her husband. **(4)**
3. In lines 8–12 ('Some nights … their prose') identify at least one contrast which suggests the persona's feeling of superiority over her guests and evaluate its effectiveness. **(2)**
4. By referring to this poem and at least one other by Carol Ann Duffy, discuss her use of an unexpected or surprise ending. **(10)**

Exercise 4 🖊

Attempt to answer questions 1, 2 and 3. Even if you have not studied Carol Ann Duffy's poetry as a specified text, answering these three questions should not be too difficult, especially when you have the text of the poem in front of you.

(Answers on page 133.)

Answer

This section takes you through a possible answer to question 4. Remember, though, that there will be many other equally acceptable answers.

4. **By referring to this poem and at least one other by Carol Ann Duffy, discuss her use of an unexpected or surprise ending. (10)**

   To make sure you answer all the parts of this last question you must do **three** *things:*

   A *You should show how your understanding of the effect of an unexpected or surprise ending to a poem makes the reader think again about the poem.*

   B *Next you should show how this technique has been demonstrated in the text in front of you.*

   C *For the 6 additional marks available you need to refer to the effect of an unexpected or surprise ending in one (or more than one) of the other poems by Carol Ann Duffy you have studied. In this case 'Valentine' could provide the material needed.*

   For example:

   A A surprise ending has the power to make the reader think again in that it can take a portrayal of something like a relationship from a purely descriptive angle, which is interesting in its own right, and move on to a new perspective which makes the reader look back at the relationship in a new light and with a greater understanding.

   B The surprise ending of 'Anne Hathaway' makes the reader look back at the happiness portrayed in the majority of the poem and suddenly see it from the perspective of the fact that her husband is dead – but that the relationship between them was so powerful that she still seems to be able to retain his memory in their bed. This somehow seems to strengthen the relationship in the reader's eyes – that it can outlive death. The ending is given an extra power technically as the last two lines form a rhyming couplet – traditionally the ending to

⇨

⇨

a Shakespearean sonnet – where the 'head'/'bed' rhyme lends force to the importance of the bed they shared in their marriage.

Parts A and B could be dealt with together, but the general idea of a surprise ending and the particular ending of this poem would both have to be covered.

C *You would be expected to make references to the other poem you have chosen to look at – in this case, 'Valentine' – showing their contribution to the effect of the surprise or unexpected ending.*

Bullet points

- The reference to 'Lethal./Its scent will cling to your fingers,/cling to your knife' seems a surprising ending to what starts out as a love poem, suggesting that their relationship may be 'murdered'.
- The promising start to the gift of the onion – 'It promises light/like the careful undressing of love' – suggests that the gift, though unusual, has more power than a conventional Valentine.
- Later in the poem the onion is seen as a symbol of an attempt to be truthful, which looks at the relationship straight on, but still sees it as cementing it with a 'fierce kiss'.
- The possessive and faithful references seem to be leading up to something perhaps positive – maybe even the suggestion of marriage in 'Its platinum loops shrink to a wedding-ring'.
- The final lines suggesting that the onion may be 'lethal' to the relationship, and that the recipient of the gift may be the one to 'kill' the relationship, cause the reader to look back at the whole poem and possibly see the hints of troubles to come right from the beginning – 'blind you', 'grief', 'for as long as we are'.

Two important ideas well explained (with references) or three of them explained in a simpler way would support an answer to the question. But it is not an easy task. You have to select relevant references and link them with the idea of the surprise ending. Another poem that could be used for this question would be 'Mrs Midas'.

Prose

Short story

The short story option from the specified Scottish texts has some of the advantages and some of the drawbacks that have already been described in the Poetry section.

The total scope of all six stories in each of the selections (George Mackay Brown and Iain Crichton Smith) is only just over 12,000 words – much shorter than a novel or a play. But again you need to have a detailed knowledge of all six of the stories for the writer you have been taught. You will be presented with an extract from one of the stories, which you have to relate to at least one other story.

There are at least **two** kinds of final 10-mark questions:

1 One is concerned with identifying a common **theme or central concern**.

2 The other is concerned with the use of a **similar technique or set of techniques**.

The first short story A, 'The Painter' by Iain Crichton Smith, concentrates on theme or central concerns in the last question.

The second short story B, 'The Crater' also by Iain Crichton Smith, concentrates on structural technique.

Hints & tips ★

If you have a choice between this Scottish text and another, you should look carefully at **all** the questions asked on **this story**. You may be quite happy with the choice of 'The Painter', but always look at the last question (in this case, question 5) to see how easily it allows you to show your knowledge of another short story by Iain Crichton Smith. Before you make up your mind finally, you should **always** have looked at Section 2 before making your choice.

(A) The Painter (extract)

As Red Roderick was drunk perhaps the advantage given him by relative youth was to a certain extent cancelled. There was however no doubt that he wished to kill the old man, so enraged was he, so frustrated by the life that tortured him. As they swung their
5 scythes towards each other ponderously, it looked at first as if they could do little harm, and indeed it was odd to see them, as if each was trying to cut corn. However, after some time – while the face of the old man gradually grew more demoniac in a renewal of his youth – he succeeded at last in cutting his son-in-law's left
10 leg so that he fell to the ground, his wife running towards him like an old hen, her skirts trailing the ground like broken wings.

But that was not what I meant to tell since the fight in itself, though unpleasant, was not evil. No, as I stood in the ring with the others, excited and horrified, I saw on the edge of the ring
15 young William with his paint-brush and canvas and easel painting the fight. He was sitting comfortably on a chair which he had taken with him and there was no expression on his face at all but a cold clear intensity which bothered me. It seemed in a strange way as if we were asleep. As the scythes swung to and fro, as the

⇨

⇒

20 faces of the antagonists became more and more contorted in the
fury of battle, as their cheeks were suffused with blood and rage,
and their teeth were drawn back in a snarl, he sat there painting
the battle, nor at any time did he make any attempt to pull his
chair back from the arena where they were engaged.

25 I cannot explain to you the feelings that seethed through me as I
watched him. One feeling was partly admiration that he should be
able to concentrate with such intensity that he didn't seem able
to notice the danger he was in. The other feeling was one of the
most bitter disgust as if I were watching a gaze that had gone
30 beyond the human and which was as indifferent to the outcome
as a hawk's might be. You may think I was wrong in what I did
next. I deliberately came up behind him and upset the chair so
that he fell down head over heels in the middle of a brush-stroke.

35 He turned on me such a gaze of blind fury that I was reminded
of a rat which had once leaped at me from a river bank, and he
would have struck me but that I pinioned his arms behind his
back. I would have beaten him if his mother hadn't come and
taken him away, still snarling and weeping tears of rage. In spite
40 of my almost religious fear at that moment, I tore the painting into
small pieces and scattered them about the earth. Some people
have said since that what I wanted to do was to protect the good
name of the village but I must in all honesty say that that was not
what was in my mind when I pushed the chair over. All that was
45 in my mind was fury and disgust that this painter should have
watched this fight with such cold concentration that he seemed
to think that the fight had been set up for him to paint, much as a
house exists, or an old wall.

Iain Crichton Smith

Questions ?

1 By close reference to the text, explain how the characterisation of Red
Roderick, and of Big Angus, and of Roderick's wife, Anna, is developed by
the detail in the first paragraph. **(3)**

2 Analyse the contribution of the first sentence in paragraph 2 to the
structure of the short story. **(2)**

3 By referring closely to the text, analyse how the description of the boy's
behaviour adds to his feeling of 'bitter disgust' in lines 29–39. **(3)**

4 '... much as a house exists, or an old wall' (lines 48–49). Give one reason
why the writer uses this phrase at this point in the story. **(2)**

5 By referring to this story and one other by Iain Crichton Smith, discuss
his presentation of a character who is 'different' in some way from those
people who surround her or him. **(10)**

This section takes you through possible answers to these questions. Remember, though, that there will be many other equally acceptable answers.

1 **By close reference to the text, explain how the characterisation of Red Roderick, and of Big Angus, and of Roderick's wife, Anna, is developed by the detail in the first paragraph. (3)**
   - Red Roderick: 'so frustrated by the life that tortured him'. This phrase suggests the origin of his violence is his sharp disappointment with his way of life.
   - Big Angus: 'the face of the old man grew gradually more demoniac in a renewal of his youth'. In temporarily overcoming the weakness of age, Big Angus is reverting to type. He is almost outside of himself – 'demoniac'.
   - Anna: 'running towards him like an old hen, her skirts trailing the ground like broken wings'. This simile reinforces her weakness and ineffectual nature, but also shows her loyalty to her husband.

2 **Analyse the contribution of the first sentence in paragraph 2 to the structure of the short story. (2)**
   The sentence acts as a turning point in the story. It moves on from the fight to what is going to be truly evil – the painter's behaviour.

3 **By referring closely to the text, analyse how the description of the boy's behaviour adds to his feeling of 'bitter disgust' in lines 29–39. (3)**
   In these lines, the writer's word choice and imagery in describing the boy emphasise the elements in the boy's behaviour that disgust him:
   - 'beyond the human'
   - 'indifferent ... as a hawk's'
   - 'gaze of blind fury'
   - 'a rat'
   - 'still snarling'
   - 'weeping tears of rage.
   Good comment on the effectiveness of three of the above would provide an answer. Remember that the reference alone does not provide any marks.

4 **'... much as a house exists, or an old wall' (lines 48–49). Give one reason why the writer uses this phrase at this point in the story. (2)**
   - The narrator sees that the boy makes no distinction between human beings and inanimate objects like a house or a wall.
   OR
   - It is a reminder of earlier in the story where the narrator admires the way the boy spends hours painting these things.

5 **By referring to this story and one other by Iain Crichton Smith, discuss his presentation of a character who is 'different' in some way from those people who surround her or him. (10)**
   *To make sure you answer all the parts of this last question you must do **three** things:*
   A *You should show your understanding of a character who is 'different' in some way from those people who surround him or her.*
   B *Next you should show how the idea of 'difference' has been dealt with in the text in front of you.*
   C *For the 6 additional marks available you need to refer to the idea of difference in one (or more than one) of the other short stories by Iain Crichton Smith you have studied. In this case 'The Red Door' could provide the material needed.*

⇨

⇨

For example:

A The character who is different serves to throw the spotlight on the society of which he/she is a part, sometimes to increase the reader's understanding of that particular character and sometimes to allow the reader to take a closer look at the surrounding society, with its faults and virtues.

B At the beginning of 'The Painter' you are told how gifted a painter he is, but there are unsettling hints about what is to come. For example, the sheep 'with its eyes eaten out by a crow' and the strange painting of a sack of flour which was hanging in a disturbing way. He seemed to have a fascination with the macabre – putting the cemetery right in the centre of the village.

Parts A and B could be dealt with together, but the general idea of the character who is different and the particular application of that idea in this short story would both have to be covered.

C *You would be expected to make references to the other short story you have chosen to look at – in this case 'The Red Door' – showing how the 'different' character is presented. You can answer this question either by the use of bullet points or in a series of linked statements. Both of these methods are shown below.*

Bullet points

- Murdo as a child is shown to be different from the other children – clumsier and seen as foolish – and so as an adult he tried to blend in, wearing the same clothes and doing what they did, but underneath there is something else.
- Murdo seems to be like everyone else – he felt he should be 'as like the other villagers as possible'.
- But he dreamed of more than that – he had an imagination which had no outlet – 'a strange volume which none could read except by means of the imagination'.
- He is not upset that his door is now red, unlike anyone else's.
- He is vaguely attracted to Mary, who doesn't care what the villagers think of her and who reads poetry – again this suggests that he actually is attracted to what is strange and different.
- The red door makes him think about his boring, conforming life: 'I have always worn these things because everybody else does', but he realises that he would really like to have something totally different, like a coloured waistcoat or jacket.
- The red door gave him confidence to be different – to go and see Mary, and not to care if the village didn't like him.
- The red door becomes a symbol for Murdo's new capacity for change.
- The symbol of the Hallowe'en masks runs through the story, and at the end he feels he has got rid of the mask.

Series of linked statements

In 'The Red Door', Murdo as a child is shown to be different from the other children – clumsier and seen as foolish – and so as an adult he tried to blend in, wearing the same clothes and doing what they did, but underneath there is something else. The writer uses the Hallowe'en masks symbolically to emphasise this. Murdo first sees them on the children, and they disguise them almost completely. Later he talks about his 'belonging had been like a Hallowe'en mask' and there is a link to Mary, who made the masks for the children.

He appears to be just like everyone else; in fact, he deliberately does what everyone else does, but he is dissatisfied – feeling that there is something beyond – 'and the earth was

⇨

⇨

painted with an unearthly glow and the sea was like a strange volume which none could read except by means of the imagination'. The writer uses this evocative language to contrast with the humdrum life that Murdo outwardly leads.

The red door is the catalyst that makes him think he could possibly be happy being different. The door seems to be linked in his mind with the only other outsider in the village, Mary, who reads poetry and doesn't particularly care what others think of her. He says: 'I have never had the courage to wear what I wanted to wear, for example a coloured waistcoat and a coloured jacket.' The red door symbolically gives him confidence to go and see Mary. 'There was pride and spirit about it. It said, 'Please let me live my own life.'

Two important ideas well explained (with references) or three of them explained in a simpler way would support an answer to the question. But it is not an easy task. You have to select relevant references and link them with the idea of 'difference'. 'Mother and Son' could also have provided a possible companion piece to 'The Painter'. The son is set apart by his mother's control over him, his movements and his life choices, which prevent him being like others in the community.

Exercise 5 ✏

Try to comment relevantly on each of the words/phrases given in the answer to question 3 on page 114. There are six examples identified by bullet points.

(Answer on page 133.)

Hints & tips ★

*If you have a choice between this Scottish text and another, you should look carefully at **all** the questions asked on **this story**. You may be quite happy with the choice of 'The Crater', but always look at the last question (in this case, question 4) to see how easily it allows you to show your knowledge of another short story by Iain Crichton Smith. Before you make up your mind finally, you should **always** have looked at Section 2 before making your choice.*

(B) The Crater (extract)

The moon shone suddenly out between two clouds and in that moment he saw it, a body covered with greenish slime, an obscene mermaid, hanging on to his rifle while the two eyes, white in the green face, shone upward and the mouth, gritted,
5   tried not to let the blood through. It was a monster of the deep, it was a sight so terrible that he nearly fell. He was about to say, 'It's no good, he's dying,' but something prevented him from saying it, if he said it then he would never forget it. He knew that. The hands clung to the rifle below in the slime. The others pulled
10   behind him. 'For Christ's sake hang on to the rifle,' he said to the monster below. 'Don't let go.' And it seemed to be emerging from the deep, setting its feet against the side of the crater, all green, all mottled, like a disease. It climbed as if up a mountainside in the stench. It hung there against the wall. 'Hold on,' he said.
15   'Hold on.' His whole body was concentrated. This man must not fall down again into that lake. The death would be too terrible. The face was coming over the side of the crater, the teeth gritted, blood at the mouth. It hung there for a long moment and then the three of them had got him over the side. He felt like cheering,

⇨

⇨
20 standing up in the light of No Man's Land and cheering. Sergeant
Smith was kneeling down beside the body, his ear to the heart. It
was like a body which might have come from space, green and
illuminated and slimy. And over it poured the merciless moonlight.

'Come on,' he said to the other two. And at that moment Sergeant
25 Smith said, 'He's dead.'

'Dead?' There was a long pause. 'Well, take him in anyway. We're
not leaving him here. We'll take him in. At least he didn't die
in the bloody lake.' They lifted him up between them and they
walked to the trench. 'I'm bloody well not crawling,' said Robert.
30 'We'll walk. And to hell with the lot of them.' He couldn't prevent
himself from swearing and at the same time despising himself for
swearing. What would Sergeant Smith think of him? It was like
bringing a huge green fish back to the lines. 'To hell with them,'
he shouted. 'This time we'll bloody well walk. I don't care how
35 light it is.' And they did so and managed to get him back into the
dugout. They laid him down on the floor and glared around them
at the silent men.

'Just like Piccadilly it was,' said Harris, who couldn't stop talking.
'As bright as day.'

40 'Shut up, you lot,' said Sergeant Smith, 'and get some sleep.'

Robert was thinking of the man he had seen reading a book in
a flash of light before they had gone in with their bayonets. He
couldn't see properly whether it had been a novel or a comic.
Perhaps it was a German comic. Did Germans have comics? Like
45 that green body emerging out of the slime, that fish. He began to
shiver and said, 'Give the men whisky if there is any.' But he fell
asleep before he could get any himself, seeing page after page of
comics set before him, like red windows, and in one there was
a greenish monster and in another a woman dancing with a fat
50 officer. Overhead the shells still exploded, and the water bounced
now and again from the craters.

'The bloody idiot,' said Sergeant Smith looking down at him. 'He
could have got us all killed.' Still, it had been like Piccadilly right
enough. Full of light. It hadn't been so bad. Nothing was as bad as
55 you feared.

Iain Crichton Smith

Questions ?

1 By referring closely to lines 1–23, analyse the ways in which the writer
creates a sense of horror about Morrison. **(4)**
2 How do Robert's words and actions in paragraphs 2 and 3 (lines 24–37)
of the extract add to our understanding of his state of mind? **(4)**
3 What is the importance of Harris's words in lines 38–39 in the context of
this extract? **(2)**
4 By referring to this short story and at least one other by Iain Crichton
Smith, discuss the effectiveness of the endings. **(10)**

Exercise 6 🖉

Attempt to answer questions 1, 2 and 3. Even if you have not studied Iain Crichton Smith's short stories as a specified text, answering these three questions should not be too difficult. It is always beneficial to try out your skills on a short piece of prose.

(Answers on pages 133–34.)

Answer

This section takes you through a possible answer to question 4. Remember, though, that there will be many, other equally, acceptable answers.

4 **By referring to this short story and at least one other by Iain Crichton Smith, discuss the effectiveness of the endings. (10)**

   *To make sure you answer all the parts of this last question you must do **three** things:*

   A *You should show how your understanding of the effectiveness of the ending in a short story.*

   B *Next you should show how this technique has been demonstrated in the text in front of you.*

   C *For the 6 additional marks available you need to refer to the effectiveness of the ending of one (or more than one) of Iain Crichton Smith's short stories. In this case 'The Telegram' could provide the material you need but, in fact, any of the stories would be possible.*

   For example:

   A An effective ending to a short story puts the story into perspective by making the reader reflect on the story as a whole, providing a conclusion relating to the central concerns of the story by providing a satisfactory ending to the central incident, and making clear important aspects of characterisation.

   B In the ending of 'The Crater', the reference to Piccadilly 'Full of light' shows a sort of admiration on the part of the experienced Sergeant Smith for the foolhardiness/bravery/bloodymindedness of his inexperienced officer Robert: 'The bloody idiot' (characterisation). The last line is also unexpected, given the fact that the horrible experience of the raid has been gruesomely described in the body of the story. It suggests an optimism – surprising in the context of a horrible war (central concern).

   Parts A and B could be dealt with together, but the general idea of the effective ending and the particular ending to this short story would both have to be covered.

   C *You would be expected to make references to the other short story you have chosen to look at – in this case 'The Telegram' – showing the effectiveness of the ending.*

Bullet points

- The opening sets up the idea that telegrams arrive apparently 'meaninglessly' or 'randomly'.
- The local elder 'clad in black' is seen as the messenger of death.
- The main body of the story concerns the relationship between the two women who fear that the telegram being brought along the street contains news of the death of one of their sons.
- Tension is built up – 'That means it can't be Roddy' – and then the Stewarts' house – 'Two houses to go'.
- The tension and fear causes the two women for an instant to share sympathies in ways that they never had before: 'And at that moment the fat woman saw'.

⇨

- The expectation that sympathy will be needed is maintained until the elder passed their houses in what seems a miraculous way.
- The ending leads to relief for the women, but their relief contrasts with the sadness of the end for the elder, whose son has been killed. 'Perhaps he was going in search of his son'.
- The ending is effective in deepening the reader's feelings about the harm that war does to the community.

Two important ideas well explained (with references) or three of them explained in a simpler way would support an answer to the question. But it is not an easy task. You have to select relevant references and link them with the effectiveness of the ending. 'The Red Door' would also provide a good answer to this question; in fact, any of the stories could be used.

Hints & tips ★

You are expected to be able to quote from other relevant parts of the short story:
- *'Perhaps he was going in search of his son'*

But you can also make reference to scenes and incidents without quoting directly:
- *the incident where the two women share sympathy with each other.*

Novel

(A) *The Cone-Gatherers* (extract)

Hidden among the spruces at the edge of the ride, near enough to catch the smell of larch off the cones and to be struck by some of those thrown, stood Duror the gamekeeper, in an icy sweat of hatred, with his gun aimed all the time at the feebleminded
5 hunchback grovelling over the rabbit. To pull the trigger, requiring far less force than to break a rabbit's neck, and then to hear simultaneously the clean report of the gun and the last obscene squeal of the killed dwarf would have been for him, he thought, release too, from the noose of disgust and despair drawn, these
10 past few days, so much tighter.

He had waited for over an hour there to see them pass. Every minute had been a purgatory of humiliation: it was as if he was in their service, forced to wait upon his masters. Yet he hated and despised them far more powerfully than he ever had liked and
15 respected Sir Colin and Lady Runcie-Campbell. While waiting, he had imagined them in the darkness missing their footing in the tall tree and coming crashing down through the sea of branches

⇨

⇨ to lie dead on the ground. So passionate had been his visualising of that scene, he seemed himself to be standing on the floor of a
20 fantastic sea, with an owl and a herd of roe-deer flitting by quiet as fish, while the yellow ferns and bronzen brackens at his feet gleamed like seaweed, and the spruce trees swayed above him like submarine monsters.

He could have named, item by item, leaf and fruit and branch, the
25 overspreading tree of revulsion in him; but he could not tell the force which made it grow, any more than he could have explained the life in himself, or in the dying rabbit, or in any of the trees about him.

This wood had always been his stronghold and sanctuary; there were many places secret to him where he had been able to fortify
30 his sanity and hope. But now the wood was invaded and defiled; its cleansing and reviving virtues were gone. Into it had crept this hunchback, himself one of nature's freaks, whose abject acceptance of nature, like the whining protestations of a heathen in front of an idol, had made acceptance no longer possible for
35 Duror himself. He was humpbacked, with one shoulder higher than the other; he had no neck, and on the mis-shapen lump of his body sat a face so beautiful and guileless as to be a diabolical joke. He was now in the wood, protected, not to be driven out or
40 shot at or trapped or trampled on; and with him was his brother, tall, thin, grey-haired, with an appearance of harsh meditation obviously false in a man who read no books and could only spell through a newspaper word by word: They had been brought into the wood: a greasy shed, hardly bigger than a rabbit-hutch, had
45 been knocked together in a couple of hours, and set up in one of Duror's haunts, a clearing amongst cypresses, where, in early summer, hyacinths had bloomed in thousands. Already, after only a week, the ground round about was filthy with their refuse and ordure. They were to be allowed to pollute every tree in the wood
50 except the silver firs near the big house.

Duror was alone in his obsession. No one else found their presence obnoxious; everybody accepted the forester's description of them as shy, honest, hard-working, respectable men …

Robin Jenkins

Hints & tips

If you have a choice between this Scottish text and another, you should look carefully at **all** the questions asked on **this novel**. You may be quite happy with the choice of The Cone-Gatherers but always look at the last question (in this case, question 5) to see what it is you have been asked to do in the context of the novel as a whole. Before you make up your mind finally, you should **always** have looked at Section 2 before making your choice.

Questions ❓

1 By referring closely to at least two examples in lines 1–10, analyse how Jenkins conveys Duror's feelings towards Calum. **(4)**
2 In lines 11–18 analyse how Jenkins creates a sense of the length of time that Duror has been waiting. **(2)**
3 By analysing the imagery of the tree in lines 24–27, show how it effectively reflects Duror's thoughts. **(2)**
4 By referring to at least one example from lines 28–50, analyse how the writer shows the importance of the wood to Duror. **(2)**
5 'Duror was alone in his obsession' (line 51). Discuss how this idea is illustrated in the extract and elsewhere in the novel. **(10)**

Exercise 7 ✏️

The first four questions are very similar to the type of questions already dealt with in the short story section. You could attempt to answer these even though you have not studied this novel in your course. The ability to understand and analyse a short passage of fiction cannot be practised too often.

(Answers on pages 134–35.)

Answer

This section takes you through a possible answer to question 5. Remember, though, that there will be many other, equally acceptable, answers.

5 **'Duror was alone in his obsession' (line 51). Discuss how this idea is illustrated in the extract and elsewhere in the novel. (10)**

*To make sure you answer all the parts of this last question you must do **three** things:*

A *You should show how your understanding of obsession has been developed.*

B *Next you should show how the idea of 'obsession' has been dealt with in the extract in front of you.*

C *For the 6 additional marks available you need to refer to the idea of obsession elsewhere in the novel.*

For example:

A The power of obsession can do enormous harm both to the obsessed and to those who surround her or him – it can never be 'private'; it will always spill out and hurt other people. It also destroys the ability of the obsessed person to act rationally and observe the normal terms of morality.

B The reference to his waiting 'for over an hour' just to see them pass, and the idea that he is 'forced' to wait on them as if they were 'his masters' suggests an irrational compulsion to spy on the brothers – in fact, an obsession.

Parts A and B could be dealt with together, but the general idea of obsession and the particular application of it in the extract would both have to be covered.

C *You would be expected to make several references to elsewhere in the novel where obsession is demonstrated.*

Bullet points

- Duror's obsession with the cone-gatherers is the most important element of the plot. It leads directly to the final tragedy of two deaths.
- When he sees the light in the brothers' hut, he breaks out into a sweat 'of revulsion'.
- At the deer drive he loses all sense of where he is or what he's doing when he kills the deer. He is 'possessed by a fury' and has to be restrained from attacking Calum.
- In the bar at Lendrick he cannot keep his mind off Calum sitting in the alcove of the pub, and he pays only superficial attention to the conversation he is supposed to be involved in.
- Roderick watches Duror watching the hut obsessively again for a long time and feels the presence of evil, although he does not understand what it is.
- Finally, Duror is compelled to kill Calum after his meeting with Graham in the wood where Duror's powerful fist is 'biting his chest like a gigantic spider' and he moves off 'stalking' towards the trees.
- After killing Calum he seems to have lost his anger but then had to kill himself because he had become so close in his obsession that he had to die too.

Two important ideas well explained (with references) or three of them explained in a simpler way would support an answer to the question. But it is not an easy task. You have to select relevant references and link them with the idea of Duror's obsession.

Hints & tips ★

You are expected to be able to quote from other relevant parts of the novel:
- *'possessed by a fury'*

But you can also make reference to scenes and incidents without quoting directly:
- *the incident where Roderick watches Duror spying.*

(B) *The Trick is to Keep Breathing* (extract)

Never mind. She smiles and says

 Well!

This is to make out the tea is a surprise though it isn't. She does it every time. We sit opposite each other because that's the way the chairs are. The chairs cough dust from under their sheets as she
5 crosses her legs, thinking her way into the part. By the time she's ready to start I'm grinding my teeth back into the gum.

HEALTH VISITOR: So, how are you/how's life/what's been happening/anything interesting to tell me/what's new?
PATIENT: Oh, fine/nothing to speak of.

10 I stir the tea repeatedly. She picks a piece of fluff off her skirt.

HEALTH VISITOR: Work. How are things at work? Coping?
PATIENT: Fine (Pause) I have trouble getting in on time, but getting better.

I throw her a little difficulty every so often so she feels I'm telling
15 her the truth. I figure this will get rid of her quicker.

HEALTH VISITOR: (Intensifying) But what about day-to-day? How are you coping?
PATIENT: OK. (Brave smile) I manage.
HEALTH VISITOR: The house is looking fine.
20 PATIENT: Thank-you. I do my best.

This is overdone. She flicks her eyes up to see and I lower mine. She reaches for a biscuit.

HEALTH VISITOR: These look nice. I like a biscuit with a cup of tea.

25 We improvise about the biscuits for a while, her hat sliding back as she chews. She doesn't like the tea. Maybe she eats so many biscuits just to get rid of the taste. ⇨

⇨ HEALTH VISITOR: Aren't you having one? They're very good.
PATIENT: No, thanks. Maybe later. Having lunch soon.

30 She goes on munching, knowing I don't want to her to be here/
that I do want her to be here but I can't talk to her.

This is the fourth time we've played this f****** game.

The first time was the worst. I went through the tea ceremony for
five minutes then tried to get the thing opened up.

35 What are you supposed to come here for? I said. She just looked.

What's it for? What are we supposed to talk about?

She said, I'm here to help you. To help you to try to get better.
I'm here to listen.

But I don't know you from a hole in the wall. I can't do it.

40 She said, You can tell me anything you like. I assure you it goes
no further and I've heard it all before.

I could hear my own breathing. I knew Dr Stead was doing his
best for me and that was why she was here. I had to try. It was
reasonable. I swallowed hard. I can't remember what I said now.
45 Whatever it was, I was in mid-flow, keeping my eyes low because
I couldn't look her in the eye. When I finished, nothing happened.
I looked up.

She was dunking a gingernut. I watched her hand rocking back
and forth, getting the saturation just right. At the crucial moment,
50 she flipped the biscuit to her mouth, sucking off the soaked part,
her tongue worming out for a dribble of tea. It missed. The dribble
ran down to her chin and she coughed, giggling. And I had forgotten
what I had to say. I knew if I opened my mouth something
terrible would dribble out like the tea, and gush down the front of
55 my skirt, over her shoes and cover the carpet like

like

like

She sucked her teeth and leaned closer, whispering.
She knew how I felt. Did I think the doctor hadn't given her case
60 notes? She knew all about my problems. Did I want her to tell me
a true story? Her niece had an accident on her bike once. And
she thought, what'll happen if Angela dies? What'll happen? But
she prayed to God and the family rallied round and they saw her
through to the other side. That's what I had to remember. She
65 knew how I felt; she knew exactly how I felt.

She keeps coming anyway. I make tea and fetch biscuits and we
forget all about that first little hiccup. This time she eats only the
coffee biscuits so I make a mental note. No more fig rolls. The way
I'm coiled is getting uncomfortable. One foot has gone to sleep
70 and my tea is coated. I put it down on the rug and straighten up.

⇨

⇨ HEALTH VISITOR: (alert to the change) Nothing else to tell me then?
PATIENT: No. Nothing special.

She looks blank and vaguely disappointed. I am not trying.

75 PATIENT: I have a friend visiting tonight. That's all.
HEALTH VISITOR: Anyone special? Going out?
PATIENT: Just the pub, have a few drinks, that kind of thing.
HEALTH VISITOR: Lucky girl. I can't remember the last time someone took me out. Lucky.

80 She smiles and stands up but guilt is spoiling the relief. I get more guilty as she waddles towards the door, tumbling crumbs from the folds of blue coat, fastening up one top button, ready for outside. My temples thunder as she touches the door and something buzzes in my ear,

85 You Always Expect Too Much.

The exhaust rattles till she curves out of sight, struggling against her bulk and the need to turn the wheel.

Janice Galloway

Questions ?

1 By referring closely to the writer's use of dialogue between Joy and the Health Visitor (lines 7–24), explain what each of them is trying to do. **(4)**
2 Referring closely to the language of lines 58–65, show how it conveys Joy's attitude to the Health Visitor. **(4)**
3 By analysing the writer's use of language in lines 66–84, show that each character is anxious for the meeting to end. **(2)**
4 There are accounts of other unsatisfactory interviews between Joy and other professionals. Choose one, or more than one, of these interviews and describe in what ways it/they are not helpful. **(10)**

Answers

This section takes you through possible answers to these questions. Remember, though, that there will be many other equally acceptable answers.

1 **By referring closely to the writer's use of dialogue between Joy and the Health Visitor (lines 7–27), explain what each of them is trying to do. (4)**
- The Health Visitor is trying to get Joy to open up about her problems by asking very general open questions – 'How are you?', 'How's life?' etc.
- She moves on to more specific questions about work, still trying to get a reaction from Joy.
- She compliments Joy on the cleanliness of the house, hoping to warm her up.
- Joy is answering in a non-committal way, lying about her state of mind – 'Oh, fine'.
- Joy throws in a little difficulty – 'I have trouble getting in on time' – so that it doesn't look too obvious that she is lying.

⇨

⇨

- Joy answers too glibly – 'I do my best' – and is almost caught out by the Health Visitor ('She flicks her eyes up to see').

2 **Referring closely to the language of lines 58–65, show how it conveys Joy's attitude to the Health Visitor. (4)**
- 'she sucked her teeth' – not an attractive action.
- 'leaned closer, whispering' suggests that she is invading Joy's personal space.
- repetition of 'She knew how I felt' emphasises just how much she did not know what Joy was feeling.
- 'Did I want her to tell me a true story?' is almost treating her like a child.
- the anecdote about the niece is so trivial that it means nothing to Joy and does nothing to help her.
- reported speech is used to suggest a distance between them, almost as if Joy is disconnected from her.

3 **By analysing the writer's use of language in lines 66–84, show that each character is anxious for the meeting to end. (2)**

Health Visitor:
- 'alert to the change' suggests that the Health Visitor has been waiting for a cue to leave.
- 'Nothing else to tell me then?' is an exit question, meaning that she can go.

Joy:
- Joy puts the cup down on the rug to give the Health Visitor a cue to leave.
- 'guilt is spoiling the relief' – Joy is desperate for her to go, but feels guilty that she feels so relieved.

The mark allocation for this question is only 2, so you would only need to make two points, but they would have to be one from each character.

4 **There are accounts of other unsatisfactory interviews between Joy and other professionals. Choose one, or more than one, of these interviews and describe in what ways it/they are not helpful. (10)**

To make sure you answer all the parts of this last question you must do **three** *things:*

A *You should show how the understanding of the fact that experience of other interviews between Joy and other professionals can be unsatisfactory has been developed.*

B *Next you should show how the nature of the unsatisfactory interview has been demonstrated in the extract in front of you.*

C *For the 6 additional marks available you need to refer to one (or more than one) example(s) of unsatisfactory interviews elsewhere in the novel.*

For example:

A The frustration caused by the inability of the two people involved to communicate on any but the shallowest level is harmful to what is supposed to be a healing process, thus showing the difficulties surrounding the outcomes of any of the 'talking therapies'.

B 'You Always Expect Too Much' suggests that Joy would really almost like to get some help from these meetings: she knows she needs help. 'I don't want her to be here/that I do want her to be here' but the situation never works.

Parts A and B could be dealt with together, but the general idea of unsatisfactory interviews and the particular example of an interview in the extract would both have to be covered.

C *You would be expected to make several references to one or more than one interview in the novel. You can answer this question either by the use of bullet points or in a series of linked statements. Both of these methods are shown below.*

⇨

⇨

Bullet points

- She has several interviews with doctors, psychiatrists and the headmaster, none of which live up to her expectations – partly her fault and partly the professional's fault.
- A hopeless interview is the one with Dr Three, after she has been in hospital for several weeks and still hasn't been given what she hoped for – a treatment to cure her.
- 'What sort of treatment do you want' is not helpful – he is supposed to be the expert. She expects to be given treatment.
- She upsets Dr Three by being vaguely cheeky when she says that the other patients have given up asking. He tells her she can leave if she doesn't think that they are doing anything for her.
- She tries asking him questions to provoke some sort of reaction, but he tells her to leave.
- Her hopes of a cure are not going to be realised by this means, and at the end of the interview she sees in her head – 'You Always Expect Too Much'.

Series of linked statements

Joy has several interviews with doctors, psychiatrists and the headmaster, none of which live up to her expectations – this is partly her fault and partly the professional's fault. She has come into the hospital, after some persuasion, as a last resort for her and she expects to be given some sort of cure for her mental state. The interview with the psychiatrist, Dr Three, is completely unsatisfactory because he will not suggest a treatment for her. She has been placing her hopes in the expertise of these health professionals but they either won't, or can't, do anything to help. And they haven't helped any of the other patients either – they have even given up asking. She tries to provoke him into a personal response by asking him how he feels. But it doesn't work. Finally she asks him, 'Why do you do this?' – if he's supposed to be a psychiatrist and he never gives anyone any treatment and nobody gets any better, what is the point? The question is not welcome – perhaps because it reveals his own failure – so he dismisses her. At that point she realises that this is like all the other interviews – it will not provide the answers. 'You Always Expect Too Much' flashes into her mind as if it was on a billboard and reminds us of all the other unsatisfactory interviews she has had.

Two important ideas well explained (with references) or three of them explained in a simpler way would support an answer to the question. But it is not an easy task. You have to select relevant references and link them with another unsatisfactory interview.

Hints & tips ★

You are expected to be able to quote from other relevant parts of the novel:
- *'You Always Expect Too Much'*

But you can also make reference to scenes and incidents without quoting directly:
- *when you refer to her dismissal by Dr Three.*

Drama

The text of the following play is interesting as it was built in a collaborative way by its first cast and the writer, John McGrath. It was subject to change depending on the venue and the audience. Not all of the play was performed every time, and sometimes the script varied, but the original intention of opening the eyes of Scottish people to the exploitation they had suffered over centuries remained the same.

The Cheviot, the Stag and the Black, Black Oil (extract)

Author's note: I was present at the second ever performance of this play at the Macrobert Arts Centre in Stirling. When the play finished, the actors talked to the audience about the play. A very old man stood up at the back and said, 'My mother told me that when she was four years old, she remembered being carried up the side of the glen in her mother's arms and watching her house burning. She told me, "You might forgive, son, but never forget."' You can imagine the electrifying effect that had on the cast and the audience.

Ghillie whistles up the Beaters

Ghillie: Any moment now sir ...

Lord Crask: Here come the grouse, Lady Phosphate –

Lady Ph: What?

5 **Lord Crask:** The grouse –

Lady Ph: Oh, how lovely – *(She gets out a sten gun.)* I find it so moving that all over the north of North Britain, healthy, vigorous people are deriving so much innocent pleasure at so little cost to their fellow human beings.

10 *Barrage. Ghillie aims Lord Crask's gun up higher, struggles with him. Lady Phosphate fires her sten from the hip. Bombs, shells, etc. Barrage ends.*

Ghillie: Oh no – Thon was a nice wee boy.

Music – guitar and mandolin begins. Lord Crask and Lady
15 *Phosphate sing a duet.*

Both: Oh it's awfully, frightfully, ni-i-ice,

Shooting stags, my dear, and grice –　　⇨

127

⇨ And there's nothing quite so righ-it-it

    As a fortnight catching trite:

20 And if the locals should complain,

    Well we can clear them off again.

    Lady Ph: We'll clear the straths

    Lord Crask: We'll clear the paths

    Lady Ph: We'll clear the bens

25 **Lord Crask:** We'll clear the glens

    Both: We'll show them we're the ruling class.

    Repeat from: 'We'll clear the straths'. Instrumental half verse.

    Lord Crask *(Speaking over the music)*: Oh they all come here, you
    know – Lady Phosphate of Runcorn – her husband's big in

30 chemicals – she has a great interest in Highland culture.

    Lady Ph: How I wish that I could paint –

    For the people are so quaint

    I said so at our ceilidh

    To dear Benjamin Disraeli.

35 Mr Landseer showed the way –

    He gets commissions every day –

    The Silvery Tay.

    Lord Crask: The Stag at Bay

    Lady Ph: The misty moor –

40 **Lord Crask**: Sir George McClure

    Both: We are the Monarchs of the Glen –

    Lady Ph: The Shepherd Boy

    Lord Crask: Old Man of Hoy

    Lady Ph: And Fingal's Cave

45 **Lord Crask:** The Chieftain Brave

    Both: We are Monarchs of the Glen

    Lord Crask: We love to dress as Highland lads

    In our tartans, kilts and plaids –

    Lady Ph: And to dance the shean trew-oo-oos

50 In our bonnie, ghillie, shoes –

    Both: And the skirling of the pi-broch

    As it echoes o'er the wee-loch

    Lord Crask: We love the games

    Lady Ph: Their funny names

⇨

⇨

55 **Lord Crask**: The sporran's swing

Lady Ph: The Highland fling

Both: We are more Scottish than the Scotch.

Lady Ph: The Camera-ha

Lord Crask: The Slainte-Vah

60 **Lady Ph**: Is that the lot?

Both: Sir Walter Scott –

We are more Scottish than the Scotch.

They become more serious. They turn their guns on the audience.

Lord Crask: But although we think you're quaint,

65 Don't forget to pay your rent,

And if you should want your land,

We'll cut off your grasping hand.

Lady Ph: You had better learn your place,

You're a low and servile race –

70 We've cleared the straths

Lord Crask: We've cleared the paths

Lady Ph: We've cleared the bens

Lady Ph: We've cleared the glens

Both: And we can do it once again –

75 **Lady Ph**: We've got the brass

Lord Crask: We've got the class

Lady Ph: We've got the law

Both: We need no more –

We'll show you we're the ruling class.

Song ends.

John McGrath

Questions ?

1 Identify one action and one phrase from lines 6–13 ('Oh how lovely … nice wee boy') which display a careless or patronising attitude to the Highlands and the Highlanders. **(2)**

2 'She has a great interest in Highland culture' (line 30). Analyse the language used by Lady Phosphate and Lord Crask in the song from lines 31–62, showing how it actually demeans Scottish culture rather than celebrates it. **(4)**

3 Analyse the language used about the Scots after the stage direction in line 63, showing how it marks a turning point in attitude. **(4)**

4 The use of music and song in this play is significant. By referring to this extract and elsewhere in the play, discuss the effect of these elements. **(10)**

Exercise 8 ✎

Attempt to answer questions 1, 2 and 3.

This is very difficult without having studied the play, because so much of its power depends on the 'performance' elements of the drama. But you could give it a go.

(Answers on page 135.)

This section takes you through a possible answer to question 4. Remember, though, that there will be many other, equally acceptable, answers.

4 **The use of music and song in this play is significant. By referring to this extract and elsewhere in the play, discuss the effect of these elements. (10)**

*To make sure you answer all the parts of this last question you must do **three** things:*

A *You should show your understanding of the significance of music in theatrical performance.*

B *Next you should show how the contribution of the music in the extract in front of you is successful.*

C *For the 6 additional marks available you need to refer to the success of music and song elsewhere in the play.*

For example:

A The power of music and song allows the emotions of an audience to be affected by more than just the words of the drama. It can set atmosphere and create changes of pace and mood to underpin the 'message' of the play.

B The use of the song here allows the use of rhyme and repetition initially to mock the attitudes and accents of the English aristocrats – 'grice' and 'trice' for example instead of 'grouse' and 'trout'. The repetition of chorus lines helps to make the sentiments clearer – for example, 'we'll clear the paths', etc. and 'we're the ruling class'.

Parts A and B could be dealt with together, but the general idea of the power of music in enhancing drama and the particular effect of the music in the extract would both have to be covered.

C *You would be expected to make several references to the use of music and song elsewhere in the play.*

Bullet points

- Important ideas are transmitted through the emotional atmosphere created by the music.
- Throughout the play song is used to create emotion in the audience. The opening of the play has Scottish fiddle music playing as the audience comes in to set the scene in a Scottish cultural setting.
- The song used in the section of the play describing the opposition to the Clearances ('The Battle of the Braes') literally gives a voice to the Highlanders, and the repetition of the chorus:
  'Oh the battle was long but the people were strong
  You should have been there that day'
  brings the audience (who are encouraged to sing along) emotionally onside with the actors.
- The use of Gaelic songs, even though only a small proportion of the audience understands the words, is evocative of a bygone age and the dying culture of the Gaels, which was speeded by the oppression of Scottish customs such as wearing tartan, using English as the only medium of education and suppressing the language altogether. In this case, the music carries the meaning, which the words spoken would not.
- The final song, which is in Gaelic, is sung, then translated into English for the audience and then sung again to provide a climax to the play.

Two important ideas well explained (with references) or three of them explained in a simpler way would support an answer to the question. But it is not an easy task. You have to select relevant references and link them with the effect of music and song.

Answers

There are three important points to make about the answers:

1 These are possible answers – not the only answers.
2 There are many more points contained in these answers than you would need to produce for a given question. Look at the mark allocation and see how many points you will have to make.
3 The **commentaries on the answers** are even more important than the answers themselves because they show the method of arriving at a good answer.

Note: it is not always repeated in every answer but:
1 A reference alone normally gains no marks. A basic comment is worth 1 mark, a well-developed comment can be worth 2 marks.
2 You must use your own words as far as possible: you should make clear you know the meaning of complex words; simple words can obviously be repeated without trying to find a synonym.

Answers

Exercise 1 (page 103)
- 'own country' suggests a sense of belonging being taken away from her, creating a sense of abandonment.
- 'fell through the fields' suggests lack of control and speed of the experience, creating a helpless feeling as if the ground were falling away from the train.
- 'the miles rushed back' – the personification of the miles suggests that each mile of distance is running away from her back to her home where she can't follow them, as if they (the miles) don't like where she is going to either.
- 'the city, the street, the house, the vacant rooms' – the climax of this series. The smallest space she is leaving is left till last, which shows how her memory of the home she is leaving is becoming concentrated on the rooms in the house where up until now she has been happy.
- 'stared' suggests that she is unhappily fixing her eyes on the only familiar object she has left.
- 'blind toy' – the fact that the toy is blind makes it seem a sad sight, or because it is blind it doesn't see what she sees – a bleak future.
- 'holding its paw' suggests that the poet is trying to gain some comfort from the touch of an old familiar object.

Exercise 2 (page 104)
- Imagery: 'All childhood is an emigration' suggests that children are uncertain enough about the world around them and how it changes without the added stress of changing homes.
- Word choice:
  - 'resigned' suggests a kind of helplessness on the part of the child.
  - 'unimagined' suggests a kind of unfamiliarity with the district, the unknown exists round every corner.
  - 'big boys eating worms' – the shocking nature of their behaviour makes the child feel different and possibly threatened by a sort of mindless cruelty.

⇨

- 'don't understand' suggests that the inability of the child to understand a new accent/dialect further increases her fear of the unknown.
- Contrast: 'some are slow'/'others are sudden' shows that no matter the circumstances, the feeling of displacement can happen in a wide variety of situations and you can't predict when – causing anxiety.
- The use of direct speech: the child's voice with the very simple words betray a sense of loss and discomfort.

Exercise 3 (page 107)

1. - 'unwind' – connotations of becoming looser, more expansive, less uptight contributes to a contented, carefree atmosphere/mood.
   - 'The kitchen filled with the smell of itself' – this image/personification suggests that the kitchen is somehow contented with what it is achieving although, of course, it is Mrs Midas who is actually doing the cooking.
   - 'relaxed' – connotations of stillness, lack of tension, also contribute to the contented mood.
   - 'steamy breath' is a continuation of the kitchen image, possibly suggesting sighing in contentment, enveloping the kitchen in a comfort blanket – a mood of well-being and calm.
   - 'gently' suggests that nothing sudden or harsh can happen – all movement is quiet and calm, suggesting contentment.
   - the sequence 'So … then … ' seems quite unrushed – nothing bad seems about to happen (it would be possible to say exactly the opposite about 'So … then' saying that it leads up to something dramatic).

   You would not be required to cover all of these examples. Two would be enough.

2. - 'So … then' seems likely to lead up to something dramatic.
   - Imagery: 'spitting out the teeth of the rich' is the first indication that things are going wrong. The corn is being compared to gold teeth, too hard to eat, and therefore inedible.
   - Word choice: 'toyed' suggests a childish delight in turning things to gold, progressing from 'his spoon' to all the cutlery on the table – a process that speeds up in a sort of terror.
   - Word choice: 'shaking hand' suggests that she is losing control.
   - Climax: from 'glass' to 'goblet' to 'golden chalice' shows the unbelievable and relentless process of things turning into gold under her very eyes, leading to her scream.

   There are 4 marks available for this answer. It would be possible to gain 4 marks by discussing two of these ideas in detail. Equally you could say something sensible about 3 or 4 of them and gain the same number of marks.

3. - 'I'd just poured a glass of wine' – informal, confidential tone.
   - 'So I opened one' – simple statement.
   - 'Now' as an introduction to the next part of the poem, carrying the reader into the story.
   - 'On.' Single sentence conveys her surprise.
   - 'I thought to myself'– again, the storyteller is being allowed to follow her thoughts.
   - 'Is he putting fairy lights in the tree? – the self-questioning makes her puzzlement believable.
   - 'I said, What in the name of God is going on?' – a natural question in the circumstances, therefore in character.
   - 'shaking hand' – betrays her nervousness.
   - 'It was then that I started to scream' – it all becomes too much for her, and this statement ends the first part of the story – we want to know what happens next.

   Again, two or three of these possible answers would be enough.

⇨

Exercise 4 (page 110)

1 • 'spinning world' suggests the whirling excitement of their relationship.
  • the list 'forests … seas' suggests that there is no limit to the delights they enjoy.
  • 'castles' suggest medieval romance.
  • 'torchlight' suggests exciting meetings at night, under cover of darkness.
  • 'clifftops' suggest an excitement caused by the imminence of danger.
  • 'seas' suggest, in area and depth, the vast areas where their love adventure could take place.
  • 'dive for pearls' suggests the precious nature of the prize they were seeking – their satisfaction in the relationship.

2 • 'words/were shooting stars that fell to earth as kisses' – Shakespeare's words were magical, full of promise and wishes that attach to a falling star.
  • 'my body now a softer rhyme/to his, now echo, assonance' sees their relationship mirrored in the symmetry of poetic structure – they reflect each other's feelings in the way that in poetry rhyming words 'match' each other or reflect, like an echo or similar sounds (assonance), creating a blending of their desires.
  • 'his touch/a verb dancing in the centre of a noun' suggests that she is brought alive by his touch in the same way that the subject of a sentence is given action by its verb.
  • The whole extended image, involving words, rhymes, assonance and verbs, is a highly appropriate one for describing the relationship between a writer and his wife.

3 • She has dreams while they 'dozed on' suggesting that life in her bed is richer and more charged with emotion than theirs.
  • She has 'Romance/and drama' while they are 'dribbling their prose' suggesting that her relationship is typified by high literary achievement whereas they are stuck in fairly ordinary, workaday prose.

Exercise 5 (page 116)

• 'beyond the human' – word choice suggests that the boy had no emotional connection.
• 'indifferent … as a hawk's' – this simile suggests that he is like an amoral savage bird and probably dangerous.
• 'gaze of blind fury' – word choice suggests that he was out of control, 'blind' in his anger. 'fury' suggests the extreme form of anger.
• 'a rat' – he is compared to another unappealing savage animal.
• 'still snarling' – unable to forget or control his anger; acting like an animal.
• 'weeping tears of rage – the tears are not of sorrow but of extreme anger which might be dangerous.

Exercise 6 (page 118)

1 Word choice:
  • 'greenish slime' suggests something rather disgustingly slippery, and of a colour associated with the idea of scum/plant/algae on the surface of the water.
  • 'two eyes, white in the green face' suggests a rather ghostly contrast between the eyes and the face – frightening, almost.
  • 'gritted' (line 4) suggests tremendous effort to hold in his life, with his teeth clamped against each other, grinding together.
  • 'emerging from the deep' suggests a slow appearance of the body – almost sinister.
  • 'mottled' suggests covered in blotches as if the result of some skin disease.
  • 'stench' suggests an extremely bad smell, all-pervasive.

⇨

⇨

Imagery:

- 'obscene mermaid' – mermaids are normally connected with half-human, half-fish creatures – the body here is human, but it is slippery and green like a fish, and 'obscene' suggests it is ugly – the opposite of a mermaid.
- 'monster of the deep' – the human body they are retrieving seems to have lost its humanity and to resemble something frightening out of a myth.
- 'like a disease' – this simile makes the body sound like something you would not want to touch because it might be contagious.
- the use of 'it' instead of 'he' to describe the man makes him less than human – difficult to relate to and an object, not a person.

2
- Robert's use of swearing suggests that he is not quite in control of himself – he realises he doesn't want to do it – 'despising himself for swearing'.
- He repeats himself a lot: 'Well, take him in anyway'; 'We'll take him in'; 'We'll walk'; 'we'll bloody well walk'; 'And to hell with the lot of them'; 'To hell with them' – possibly trying to convince himself that that's what they have to do – showing his frustration with the man's death and his anger at the enemy.
- His insistence on taking the body back is basically irrational but, having already put themselves in danger, he doesn't want it to be for nothing – the dignity of the corpse matters.
- His refusal to crawl suggests that he won't demean himself – in a way he is defying the enemy to do its worst.

3
- He is amazed at the daring of walking back in the full light of the shells.
  and/or
- This line prepares the way for the last lines in the extract where Sergeant Smith also mentions the light and Piccadilly.

Exercise 7 (page 120)

1
- 'icy sweat of hatred' suggests the extent of the hate – it is almost like an illness.
- 'feebleminded hunchback' – both of these imperfections add to Duror's revulsion.
- 'grovelling' suggests disgust at the scrabbling around uncontrollably.
- 'obscene squeal' – the revulsion Duror feels is against some gross obscenity that has the capacity to offend.
- 'noose' suggests that Duror is trapped by his own obsession with Calum, almost to the extent that he can hardly breathe.
- 'disgust'/'despair' – both of these words sum up his hatred and revulsion at Calum's deformities.

2
- The repetition of 'waited' and 'wait' adds to the sense of time passing.
- 'over an hour' – when added to the idea of minutes in the next sentence this makes the time seem very long drawn-out.
- 'every minute' suggests that each minute has seemed much longer, emphasising the extent of the wait.
- 'purgatory' in its religious context is the place where people with sins on their conscience had to spend an infinity of time before being admitted to heaven.
- 'wait upon his masters' has two meanings – not just the time, but the suggestion that he is their servant. This adds to Duror's feeling of endlessness.

3
- Duror can recognise that his feelings of disgust are growing in him as a tree grows, little by little, in all parts of his mind – the equivalent of the leaf, fruit and branch, reaching all parts of his being.
- He can't identify why it is growing; he doesn't understand, but feels its power.

⇨

4 • 'the wood was his 'stronghold and sanctuary' – a place where he felt secure and able to retreat from problems.
  • 'its cleansing and reviving virtues were gone' – all the healing that he depended on the wood for was lost because he saw it as now 'invaded and defiled' as if the brothers were enemies out to destroy his peace.
  • the contrast between the clearing with 'hyacinths' and the 'greasy shed' which now occupied it causes him distress.
  • 'They were to be allowed to pollute every tree in the wood' shows his anger at his wood being invaded.

Exercise 8 (page 129)
1 • Action: the careless shooting of 'the wee boy'.
  • Phrase: 'the north of North Britain' doesn't even recognise Scotland as a separate country, only a region of Britain.
  or (possibly)
  • The rest of the speech shows little understanding of the realities of Highland life.
2 • 'quaint' suggests subjects/objects to be studied with curiosity/amusement.
  • 'we are the Monarchs of the Glen' – reference to typical 'Highland scenery' pictures.
  • they (the English) are assuming the superior position.
  • 'dress as Highland lads' suggests belittling the Highlanders by perceiving them as young and unimportant.
  • 'bonnie, ghillie, shoes' – ghillie shoes are workwear for Highlanders but demoted to dance duties by the English dancing Highland dances.
  • Rhyme of 'pi-broch' with 'wee-loch' creates humour and thus trivialises the pibroch, which is the term for the 'great music' of Scotland.
  • 'funny names' – trivialises the traditional clan names.
  • Scotch (rather than Scottish) which by the nineteenth century was seen by the Scots as an English word used in a patronising manner.
  Any four of these with a reasonable comment showing how they demean the Scots.
3 • 'grasping' suggests the Scots are greedy in wanting to own their own land (anti-Scots).
  • 'low' suggests inferiority.
  • 'servile' suggests only fit for a lower level of society.
  • 'cleared' – removed the Scots as a hindrance to their (the aristocrats') use of the land, or repetition of 'cleared' suggesting their power to do anything they like.
  • 'brass' – the English have the money, not the Scots.
  • 'class' – they are 'upper' class and therefore superior to the ordinary Highlander.
  • 'law' – they have the forces of the laws of property, etc. on their side.
  • 'ruling class' – they have the power, not the Scots.
  Any four of these with a reasonable comment showing their superior, non-compromising attitude to their hold on to their land and rights.

Section 2: Critical Essay

Section 2 is worth 20 marks, and having completed Section 1 you should have 45 minutes left!

Section 2 requires you to write **one** Critical Essay on a previously studied text from Drama, Prose, Poetry, Film and TV Drama or Language Study. There are two restrictions on what you can and cannot do:

- You must not use the same **text** twice.
- Each of your answers must be on a different **genre**.

For example, if you have answered on Scottish poetry in Section 1, you cannot write your critical essay on poetry of any kind, Scottish or English.

How you approach your choice in Section 2 will depend on which texts you have been taught and which you have prepared for the exam.

If you had two or more Scottish specified texts to choose from, you will have balanced your choice between what seemed the most suitable question in Section 1 against what you are left with as the questions you must now choose from in Section 2.

There is some psychological evidence to suggest that if you very quickly scan the questions in Section 2 before getting down to answering Section 1, then some part of your brain might have been working away at clarifying your choice for Section 2 while the 'active' part of your brain has actually been busy answering the questions in Section 1. You might like to try this to see if it works for you.

When you have completed your answer to Section 1, you should read **all** the questions in **each** part of Section 2 that apply to you. For example, if you have just completed an answer on *Sunset Song*, and you have studied a play and poems but **not** Film and TV or Language, then you should look at questions 1–3 and 10–12.

Preparation for the Critical Essay questions involves both mastering **essential skills** and acquiring **good knowledge** of your texts.

Essential skills

1 Show knowledge and understanding of the chosen text.
2 Construct a relevant argument.
3 Select evidence to support your argument.
4 Analyse the effect of language/filmic techniques.
5 Engage with the text and the question.
6 Evaluate the effectiveness of the text with respect to the question.
7 Write in a technically accurate way.

If you neglect skill 7, and write an essay that fails to meet the minimum requirements for technical accuracy, then the essay cannot gain more than 9 marks out of 20, no matter how good its content is.

1 Show knowledge and understanding of the chosen text

Knowledge is the first basic requirement – you should know your text thoroughly. There is really no major skill required for that except a bit of memory work and revision.

Knowledge covers aspects of the text such as who the characters are, what happens – the events and where – in which period/society/place/country. For some poems this list may be slightly different, but even there the questions *Who?*, *What?*, *Where?* and *When?* will generally apply.

Understanding requires a bit more skill. The characters and events don't just happen in a vacuum; they will be 'concerned' with some aspect of life. What we call the 'central concerns' or sometimes the 'theme' of the text are those aspects that make literature worth reading. They expand our minds, our sympathies and our emotional capacity. They let us watch, appreciate and learn from the acting out of parts of the human drama in our minds. They give us what is called 'vicarious experience'. We learn how to put ourselves in others' shoes, and learn a little about life and how it is lived outside our own immediate environment/family/society/generation. At the end of your reading you have to be able to answer questions such as *How?* and *Why?*

For example, in a romantic novel the events may describe the ups, downs, misunderstandings and reconciliations of a central couple, but the central concerns could be any of a multitude of suggestions: the effects of the modern work/life balance; the tyranny of psychological dependency within a relationship; the strains of financial inequality between the partners; the liberating of a relationship from the constraints of society; the value of mutual support in adversity… and it is those central concerns that make us value a text.

2 Construct a relevant argument

We have come across the idea of an 'argument' twice already: once when discussing discursive writing in Chapter 1 (page 3) and again on page 35 when working on your reading skills. The concept is exactly the same in Critical Essays.

You have been asked a question about a text and you have to create a convincing series of points that answer that question. The chances are that each point is going to be contained in a paragraph, and that there will be links between these paragraphs that move towards your conclusion. For the purposes of exemplification, we will use the following synopsis of a rather limited imaginary novel.

Hints & tips

The SQA's definition of technical accuracy for the Critical Essay is: There will be *few* errors in spelling, grammar, sentence construction, punctuation and paragraphing. The essay will be capable of being understood at first reading.

The Tale of X and Y

Character X lives in a cottage several miles from of a small village. He is generally unsociable – does not invite anyone to his house. He is regarded in the village as a bit eccentric – he roams the countryside at night surrounded by his dogs, but is never seen outside during the day. The people of the village are therefore inclined to make up rumours about his past life. His family has disowned him because he is supposed to have been the reason for the loss of some family property. This is not entirely true – the property was conned out of him by character Y as part of a scam investment scheme. X had hoped to help his youngest sister to a new life in Canada. He is hiding her mistakes from the rest of the family, but can be pressured by Y who knows the whole story. Y has lied to X's family in order to keep him from being reunited with them. Y has to keep the family 'sweet' because he wants to marry into the family and gain control of their business, which is in opposition to his.

Example 1

With this imaginary novel in mind, look at the following question.

(?) Question

- Choose a novel in which a main character is isolated from his or her society. Explain the reasons for this isolation and discuss to what extent the character's personality and actions are responsible for it.

The argument could look something like this:

Character X is isolated – give examples of his isolation – lack of friends – remote house, etc.

The writer establishes reasons for isolation:
- *could be because he's 'different'*
- *possibly quarrelled with others*
- *hiding a secret*
- *rejected by his family because lies have been told about him.*

Discussion:
- *on the one hand – caused his own problems by his actions/personality*
- *on the other hand – badly treated by society, both by village and family*
- *writer has succeeded in convincing the reader one way or another*
- *on balance: more to blame or less to blame?*

This sketch of an answer provides a relevant argument. It will, incidentally, have covered the other essential skills below.

3 Select evidence to support your argument

You will have provided evidence of setting, events, etc. to back up each of the points made in the sketch of the answer above, you haven't included anything irrelevant to the question.

4 Analyse the effect of features of language

You will have done this because you have been dealing with characterisation and central concerns throughout, and possibly with setting and dialogue.

5 Engage with the text and the question

You will have faced the question head on and used your knowledge of the text to demonstrate how you have reached your conclusion.

6 Evaluate the effectiveness of the text with respect to the question

In your discussion of the extent to which the writer convinces you, for example, to be sympathetic or unsympathetic with the main character, you will have shown that you have made an evaluation of the text.

7 Write in a technically accurate way

After all that, you just have to check the accuracy of your writing – this is important because if it doesn't measure up to the definition of technical accuracy (page 137), you will fail.

Example 2

If we look at another question using the same imaginary text as on page 138, the argument will be of a totally different shape.

? Question

- Choose a novel with an incident involving two main characters that creates a turning point in the novel. Describe the incident and show to what extent the outcome for each character makes a satisfactory ending to the novel.

Hints & tips

To answer any of the questions in Section 2, you may use:
- a specified Scottish text in Section 2, as long as it is from a different genre from the question you answered in Section 1
- any other Scottish text you have been taught in a different genre
- any text in English (including in translation) and from any period in a different genre
- film or television drama from anywhere in the world.

The argument could look something like this:

Character X confronts character Y and informs him that he (X) is going to tell the whole story of the scam and his sister to his family.

So, Y:

- *uses X's eccentric personality and his supposed past misdemeanours to discredit him*
- *convinces the family to reject X*
- *gains something he wants – money/woman?*

but

- *perhaps not what he thought it would be (guilt taints his future success)*
- *character X tries to reinstate himself with his family*

but

- *because of Y's lies is rejected*

therefore

- *X slips back into isolation even more damaged than before.*

Conclusion: the writer has shown that each of the characters has flaws and, although Y may think he has won, both deserve some part in their fates.

This sketch of an answer provides a relevant argument and again you have dealt with the other essential skills below.

3 Select evidence to support your argument

The selection of evidence is different. Very little material from before the incident is used. Character Y's part has to be dealt with, as well as character X's part and the family situation gains much more prominence.

You will have provided evidence to back up each of the points made in the sketch of the answer above, but you haven't included anything irrelevant to the question.

4 Analyse the effect of features of language

You will have done this because you have been dealing with characterisation and central concerns throughout, and also conflict/contrast.

5 Engage with the text and the question

You will have faced the question head on and used your knowledge of the text to demonstrate how you have reached your conclusion.

6 Evaluate the effectiveness of the text with respect to the question

In your discussion of the extent to which the writer convinces you that they deserve their fates, you will have shown that you have made an evaluation of the text.

These **two** examples of **very different essays** on the same imaginary text should illustrate three important pieces of advice about answering questions:

1 There is **no point in swotting up a possible critical essay in advance** of seeing the questions.

2 **Analysis is not an add-on or a list of techniques** that have to be covered: relevant analysis occurs throughout your essay, when you are discussing the effectiveness of characterisation or a central concern in the course of your answer.

3 **There is no formula** that works for all texts and all questions.

Acquiring good knowledge of your texts

This involves three stages: **collecting**, **organising** and **learning**.

In the pages above we have looked at the basic skills needed to answer a question, but you can't begin to select the relevant material if you don't know your text really well and, more importantly, can remember it.

Stage 1 Collecting your materials

Your materials will include the following:

a) **The primary source** is the text itself. There is no substitute for reading the text, but the reading must be active, not passive. Active reading involves reading the text again for the specific purpose of making notes on the main characters, or for looking for useful quotations. Passive reading would simply involve reading the text through without any purpose to keep your brain alert. It is useful to have a pencil in your hand as you are reading a text, either to make notes or to mark (lightly if it's a school book!) important pages to return to.

b) **Your notes on the text** – notes you have taken or been given in class and notes you have made later. The notes you have made for yourself will be more useful than other people's notes because you will have had to understand what you are writing down, whereas you might not exactly understand the notes your friend has taken.

c) **Your memory of what other people have said about the text**, what you feel about the text, any discussions you have had on the text.

Useful ideas come up in discussion, but if you don't write them down at the time, you may forget what was said.

d) **Commercially produced notes** – but make sure that you understand what the writer is saying. Don't quote an opinion if you don't know what it means. You are likely to betray your ignorance.

e) **Notes you have found in your research on the internet** – but remember to check the credentials of the site you happen to be looking at. There will be simple stuff that you can understand, which might be wrong, or there may be complicated criticism that you don't understand fully.

f) **Essays you have written about the text** – but these are less useful than you would thinks, because they are not answers to the question you will be asked in the exam.

Stage 2 Organising your materials

Basic organisation means having all these notes available in a large file, but there are ways of sorting the material and your thoughts at the same time.

a) **Lists and tables**

One of the simplest methods is simply to gather your ideas into lists under basic headings:

- **Who?** – characters
- **What?** – the events/incidents of the play/story/poem/film
- **How?** – the techniques: structure/narrative point of view/language, etc.
- **Why?** – the questions we ask of the text: what is it really 'about' – its central concerns
- **Where?** – setting in place
- **When?** – setting in time.

A suggested version of this method is illustrated on page 143. It can be adapted for all genres except non-fiction. An example for non-fiction is given on page 144.

b) **Diagrams**

Another simple method is to use a **spider diagram**. This suits people who are more spatial in their thinking and less likely to remember lists. The key is only to add to the diagram when you gain more knowledge of your text as you go through the year.

An example diagram is illustrated on page 144. This example can be adapted to suit novels, short stories, drama, film and TV studies. A second version more suited to poetry is shown at the top of page 145.

An example for non-fiction is given at the foot of page 145.

Table for all genres except non-fiction

WHO?	WHAT?	HOW?	WHY?	WHERE/WHEN?
MAIN CHARACTERS	**PLOT**	**STRUCTURE**	**QUESTION THE TEXT**	**SETTING**
1 Name	**1 Opening: introduction of characters**	Chapters/scenes/sequences/acts/incidents/flashbacks (if important)	What is the text 'about': its central concerns?	Place
a) Relationships/conflicts			● social	
b) Main characteristics			● political	Society
c) Character development	**2 Turning points**	**CLIMAX/END/DÉNOUEMENT** (effectiveness)	● historical	
			● moral	Time
2 Name	**3 Key incidents**	**NARRATIVE** (1st/3rd/dual/framed/narrator/(un) reliable, (if important))	● emotional	
a)			● psychological	Period
b)			● etc.	
c)	**4 Ending/dénouement**	**TECHNIQUES/FEATURES/ NOVEL/SHORT STORY**		
		● language		
3) Name, etc.		● tone		
		● register	**IMPORTANT QUOTATIONS**	**IMPORTANT FOR CHARACTER?**
		● symbolism		
		● mood	PLUS → FILM/TV DRAMA	**IMPORTANT FOR CENTRAL CONCERNS?**
IMPORTANT QUOTATIONS	**IMPORTANT QUOTATIONS**	● atmosphere.	● mise en scene	
			● editing	
	DRAMA ← PLUS		● use of camera	**POSSIBLE QUOTATIONS**
MINOR CHARACTERS	● dialogue		● etc.	
Names/relationships	● soliloquy			
	● aspects of staging			
	● etc.			

Diagram for fiction/drama/film

Diagram for poetry

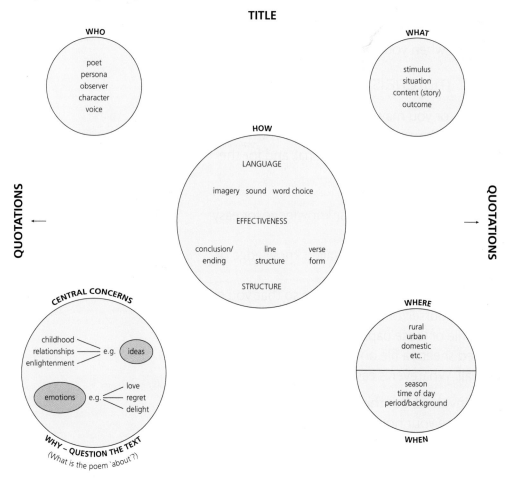

Table for non-fiction

WHO?	WHAT?	HOW?	WHY?	WHERE/WHEN?
Names	Topic	Narrative voice	Purpose/central concerns:	**Place:** geographic familiar exotic etc.
		Writer's stance	● social	
			● political	
Characteristics	Events	Sources	● historical	
			● educational	
			● moral	**Time:**
		Evidence	● etc.	period of history type of society etc.
	Conclusion			
		Technique/features:		
		● language		
		● tone		
		● rhetoric		
QUOTATIONS	**QUOTATIONS**	**QUOTATIONS**	**QUOTATIONS**	**QUOTATIONS**

There are three advantages of structuring notes in any of these forms:

- You have to think hard about your text to fill them in.
- The act of filling them in fixes them in your mind.
- They can be quickly surveyed when you come to revise.

Stage 3 Learning your materials

If you look around you will find, or you may have been taught, various kinds of study skills to help you with your learning/revision. The important thing is that you are learning the right material, and for the Critical Essay you have to know:

a) the content of your text

b) the possible ways in which you can classify your knowledge for easy selection

c) some quotations for use as evidence of your detailed knowledge of the text.

These three things should be in a readily accessible form so that you can quickly survey it all and remind yourself of the main ideas. This material should not be buried in a big file of loose papers, but organised on cards, diagrams, coloured highlighted sheets, a file on your PC (backed up!) or papered to your bedroom wall. Whatever is easiest for you.

There is some memory work involved, but the real work is done in the thinking time you put in to create your notes. Other people's notes won't do. The words have to pass through **your** brain on the way from the text to the paper to be of any use to you.

Summary 👍

1 Organising your material means you are actively engaged in learning. You are not just passively reading through your text – again!
2 Have your notes in an easily accessible form for quick scanning and revising.

Advice about quotations

Memorable quotations are likely to be quite short. It is better to have a number of short quotations that you have a chance of remembering than two or three long quotations.

Try to make your quotations do more than one task. A quotation revealing character could also be useful in talking about a central concern. And a quotation dealing with a crucial point in the text will probably be about plot character and central concerns.

When you choose your important quotations for your notes, you are actually working to deepen your understanding of the text. It is probable that you will not use all the quotations you have chosen, because the question you answer will usually require some selection of your material (including your quotations), but the effort will not have been wasted.

You should perhaps aim for about seven or eight really useful quotations per text. Poetry maybe requires a little more detail.

A very short quotation is easily incorporated into a sentence as evidence. (see the example from *Macbeth* on page 157). All you need to do is put quotation marks round the actual words quoted. If the quotation you want to use is longer than that – maybe two lines of poetry – then you should start a new line for the beginning of the quotation, use quotation marks and start a new line after the quotation (see the example from 'Church Going' on page 154). Watch your punctuation after a quotation. Often, you want to say 'This shows … ' which is the beginning of a new sentence, so 'This' needs to start with a capital letter.

Now that you know the material, we can start applying your hard-won knowledge to the exam paper in front of you. The next section looks at how best to use your knowledge with respect to:

- **reading the questions**
- **choosing the questions**
- **answering the questions.**

Reading the questions

There are two parts to each of the questions. The important part – the **real question** – is the **second part**. The first part is just an introduction defining the texts that will be suitable for the question.

Example 1

Choose a novel or short story in which there is a key incident of high tension between two of the characters.

Describe the incident fully and discuss to what extent the outcome of the incident affects the fate of the characters in the course of the novel.

The first part gets you to think if your novel has such an incident in it. As most novels involve conflict of some sort, it is highly probable that your novel will 'fit'.

But the **second part** is the **real question**. It tells you what you have **actually to do**, in this case:

- 'Describe the incident fully' suggests that you have to know this part of the novel extremely well so that you can refer to it in detail.
- 'Discuss to what extent' is another demand on you. It's not just 'what happens to each of the characters', but the balance between 'what happens to each of the characters because of the conflict' and 'what happens to them because of something else'.

Perhaps the real question – the second part – is harder than you thought when you looked simply at the introduction to the question.

Example 2

Choose a play in which a distortion of the truth (such as lies, disguise or mistaken identity) causes problems for one of the main characters.

Briefly explain what the distortion of the truth is and then discuss how the dramatist's presentation of the character's problems enhances your understanding of character in the play as a whole.

In the second part:

- 'Briefly explain' is just asking you to define the nature of the distortion and what problems it causes.
- 'dramatist's presentation' – this is really asking you about characterisation and how the character copes with the problem – successfully or unsuccessfully, for example.
- 'enhances your understanding of character in the play as a whole' means you have to put this 'character/problem' idea into the context of the play as a whole. What effect, for example, does it have on the outcome? What does the exploration of the idea have to tell you about a central concern of the play?

Example 3

Choose a novel or short story in which a specific feature such as setting, structure, narrative voice or symbolism is an important feature of the novel or short story.

Discuss how the writer uses this feature in the novel or short story and how it enhances your appreciation of the text as a whole.

In the first part the list of features is an 'open' list – 'feature such as' suggests that you can use any of the features of fiction you choose in order to answer this question.

In the second part:

- 'Discuss how the writer uses this feature' is fairly straightforward.
- '[Discuss] how this feature…enhances your appreciation of the text as a whole' means that you need to show how the use of, for example, symbolism deepens your response to the text by possibly creating something of wider significance to underline one of the central concerns. For example, the conch in *Lord of the Flies* becomes inextricably fused with the whole central concern of democracy versus dictatorship.

A number of common words and phrases crop up in typical Critical Essay questions.

- ✓ *describe the incident fully*
- ✓ *discuss to what extent*
- ✓ *briefly explain*
- ✓ *dramatist's/ novelist's/poet's/ writer's presentation*
- ✓ *enhances your understanding of X in the play as a whole*
- ✓ *enhances your appreciation of the text as a whole*
- ✓ *discuss how the writer uses this feature*
- ✓ *discuss how the poet's exploration of*
- ✓ *deepened your understanding*
- ✓ *by referring in detail*
- ✓ *how the writer creates*
- ✓ *how the writer conveys*
- ✓ *adds to your understanding of the central concerns/ appreciation of the text as a whole*
- ✓ *makes you aware of (by use of characterisation, incident, gradual revelation, etc.).*

Make sure that you are familiar with what each instruction asks you to do.

Example 4

Choose a poem in which the poet explores one of the following states of mind: depression, indecision, optimism, celebration.

Discuss how the poet's exploration of the state of mind has deepened your understanding of it.

In the second part:

- 'Discuss how the poet's exploration of' means you must look at the ways in which the poet opens up the idea of the state of mind.
- 'deepened your understanding' means you need to discuss how the poem created new insight for you about the state of mind.

Choosing the questions

You have to choose **one** question in **Section 2** and it must be from a **different** genre from the one you answered in Section 1 – Scottish texts.

Drama, fiction and poetry

Below is a sample of Section 2 questions on drama, fiction and poetry to illustrate the task of choosing the best question for your text(s). Questions 7, 8 and 9 (non-fiction) and 13, 14 and 15 (film and television drama) are given on pages 160–61.

Questions ?

Drama

1 Choose a play in which one scene brings about a reversal of fortune for one of the characters.

   By referring in detail to this scene, discuss to what extent the results of the reversal in fortune makes the character's fate inevitable.

2 Choose a play that has as one of its main concerns loss – such as loss of respect, honour or status.

   Briefly explain what the loss is and discuss how the dramatist's exploration of this loss is important to your appreciation of the play as a whole.

3 Choose a play that deals with a conflict such as that between families, generations, couples or social classes.

   Describe the conflict and discuss to what extent you find the outcome of the conflict satisfying in terms of the play as a whole.

Prose: fiction

4 Choose a novel or short story in which there is a conflict based on power, love or wealth.

   Explain how the conflict affects the characters and discuss how the writer explores the idea of power, love or wealth in the text as a whole.

5 Choose a novel or short story that has a powerful ending.

   Discuss to what extent you feel that the ending is a satisfactory outcome to the novel or short story. ⇨

6 Choose a novel or short story in which a central character seems restless, discontented or searching for something.

Discuss how the writer makes you aware of the character's situation, and discuss to what extent the character achieves peace of mind by the end of the novel.

Prose: non-fiction

Questions 7, 8 and 9 are on page 160.

Poetry

10 Choose a poem in which the poet/persona experiences a moment of revelation or understanding.

Describe what the moment was about and discuss how the experience or revelation is important to the poem as a whole.

11 Choose a poem in which the poet creates a convincing character.

Discuss how the poet, by skilful use of technique, brings the character alive in a convincing way.

12 Choose a poem which takes a disillusioned or pessimistic view of life.

Discuss how effectively the disillusionment or pessimism is revealed by the poet's treatment of the subject.

Note: it is perfectly possible that in any selection of poetry questions, there might be one involving your knowledge of two poems.

Film and television drama

Questions 13, 14 and 15 are on pages 160–61.

Let's assume that you have answered Section 1 – Scottish text by doing a text from the Poetry genre.

Remember

You might have answered on 'Originally' by Carol Ann Duffy. That means that you can't use:

☞ 'Originally'
☞ another poem by Carol Ann Duffy
☞ another poem from the specified selection of Scottish texts
☞ a poem at all – Scottish or English.

As well as the poetry you have just answered on in Section 1, let's assume you have studied both a novel and a play, so you now have to look at the first six questions in Section 2 to see which one of these six questions is best for you.

? Question 1

Choose a play in which one scene brings about a reversal of fortune for one of the characters.

If you look only at the first part of the question, you can probably think of a scene in the play you have studied which fits that definition. But, as described above, you must look at what you are being asked to **do** in the second part.

By referring in detail to this scene, discuss to what extent the results of the reversal in fortune makes the character's fate inevitable.

You probably do know how the scene affects the fate of a character, but can you refer to it **in detail**?

What looked an easy choice because you had a play that 'fitted' may turn out to be a bit more difficult, and so it might not be the best choice for you.

? Question 2

Choose a play that has as one of its main concerns loss – such as loss of respect, honour or status.

This question might be better. If your character has suffered a 'reversal of fortune', it is likely that this will have involved a loss of some kind, so your play will 'fit'.

Now look at the **real** question, the one you actually have to answer:

Briefly explain what the loss is and discuss how the dramatist's exploration of this loss is important to your appreciation of the play as a whole.

You don't have the problem in this question of having to know a particular scene in detail so, on the whole, it is probably an easier choice than question 1.

You would now look at question 3 to see what it offers – remembering to look carefully at the second part of the question.

? Question 3

Choose a play that deals with a conflict between families, generations, couples or social classes.

Describe the conflict and discuss to what extent you find the outcome of the conflict satisfying in terms of the play as a whole.

If this question fits your text, you would have two terms to deal with:

- 'Describe' is fairly straightforward, and gives you an easy entry to your essay.
- 'satisfying' – this doesn't necessarily have anything to do with a 'happy' ending. It means that the ending of the conflict brings a sense of 'rightness' – that the characters have reached their proper fate or destiny. For example, Romeo and Juliet both die at the end of Shakespeare's play, which is tragic and wasteful of two young lives, but the impossibility of each living without the other after such a passionate and committed love makes the ending 'right' – and the two feuding families have made their peace.

? Question 4

Choose a novel or short story in which there is a conflict based on power, love or wealth.

Explain how the conflict affects the characters and discuss how the writer explores the idea of power, love or wealth in the text as a whole.

The key point to consider here is if a conflict of this kind exists. If it does, you then have to be able to 'explain how …' and 'discuss how the writer explores …' in the light of 'the text as a whole'.

? Question 5

Choose a novel or short story that has a powerful ending.

Discuss to what extent you feel that the ending is a satisfactory outcome to the novel or short story.

The key point to consider here is if the ending is powerful. If it is, you then have to be able to 'discuss to what extent you feel that the ending is a satisfactory outcome…' Remember that 'satisfactory' does not mean 'happy' – see notes on question 3 on page 151.

? Question 6

Choose a novel or short story in which a central character seems restless, discontented or searching for something.

Discuss how the writer makes you aware of the character's situation, and discuss to what extent the character achieves peace of mind by the end of the novel.

The key point to consider here is if there is a central character who seems 'restless, discontented or searching for something'. If there is, you then have to consider the phrases in the second part of the question:

- 'makes you aware of …'
- 'to what extent …'
- '… by the end of the novel'.

Hints & tips ⭐

Remember that the first part of the question is just an introduction defining the texts that will be suitable for the question.

*In the second part, and **only** in the second part of the question, if you think it helps, you could underline or use a highlighter to mark the important instructions. If you do it **only** for the second part of the question then you will be able to see the real task ahead of you, which will help you to come to a conclusion about your choice of question.*

If you have only one other text left after Section 1, you only have to look at the three relevant questions in that text's genre.

Answering the questions

The **six points** below will help you to answer the questions:

1. **Opening paragraph** – this should signal what the main thrust of your line of thought is going to be. It should not:
   - simply repeat the question
   - make statements such as 'I am going to discuss …'
   - list techniques or features (unless specifically asked for in the question). This practice may weaken your essay because it dictates a mechanical structure that does not allow you the flexibility to create an argument. It can cause you to lose sight of the central concerns. The discussion of techniques should take place naturally in the course of developing a line of thought in the answer.

2 **Concluding paragraph** – this should reach the logical end-point of your argument, e.g. 'Hamlet has finally succeeded in avenging his father's death, although at a heavy price'. It should not:
- simply restate the question
- make statements such as 'I have shown how …' If your line of thought is sound, you will have shown this. And if your line of thought is not sound, a statement such as this will not make it so.

3 **Reordering/selecting your material** – most questions demand a degree of this.
- Some questions will have a focus which means that some of the material you have at your disposal will be not be needed.
- Some questions demand that you start from the middle of the text, or even from the end.

4 **Central concern(s)** – all questions require you to show your understanding of the central concern(s) of the text, even where this is not spelt out in the question.

5 **Quotation/reference**
- In shorter texts, such as poems, you are expected to be able to quote and comment readily from important parts of the poem or short story which are relevant to your answer.
- In longer texts, reference can be made to the text by means of quotation or by describing specific events or incidents. Close analysis of particular words and phrases is rarely necessary. There may be times in a more 'technical' question on a novel or in poetry or film where detailed (and meaningful) analytical comment is appropriate. The question itself will make it clear if this is needed.

6 **Technical features** – there is a box at the top of each genre that reminds you of a number of features of the genre. The list is an open list – it says 'such as' – so any other features that you wish to comment on are entirely acceptable, if they are relevant to the question you have been asked. They are not intended to be a list of items that you 'should' put into your essay. See point 1 above and also *Hints & tips* on page 141.

Remember

Don't forget to check your technical accuracy (see page 137).

The following pages give three demonstrations of these six points, using question 10 (poetry), question 3 (drama) and question 5 (prose: fiction) from the sample question bank on pages 149–50.

Example 1 Poetry

For this example we will look at 'Church Going' by Philip Larkin. You may not have come across this poem before in class, but if you read it now you should find that you can see how the question should be tackled – and you will have the pleasure of reading a good poem.

Church Going

Once I am sure there's nothing going on

I step inside, letting the door thud shut.

Another church: matting, seats, and stone,

And little books; sprawlings of flowers, cut

5   For Sunday, brownish now; some brass and stuff

Up at the holy end; the small neat organ;

And a tense, musty, unignorable silence,

Brewed God knows how long. Hatless, I take off

My cycle-clips in awkward reverence.

10   Move forward, run my hand around the font.

From where I stand, the roof looks almost new –

Cleaned, or restored? Someone would know: I don't.

Mounting the lectern, I peruse a few

Hectoring large-scale verses, and pronounce

15   'Here endeth' much more loudly than I'd meant.

The echoes snigger briefly. Back at the door

I sign the book, donate an Irish sixpence,

Reflect the place was not worth stopping for.

Yet stop I did: in fact I often do,

20   And always end much at a loss like this,

Wondering what to look for; wondering, too,

When churches will fall completely out of use   ⇨

⇒ What we shall turn them into, if we shall keep

A few cathedrals chronically on show,

25 Their parchment, plate and pyx in locked cases,

And let the rest rent-free to rain and sheep.

Shall we avoid them as unlucky places?

Or, after dark, will dubious women come

30 To make their children touch a particular stone;

Pick simples for a cancer; or on some

Advised night see walking a dead one?

Power of some sort will go on

In games, in riddles, seemingly at random;

35 But superstition, like belief, must die,

And what remains when disbelief has gone?

Grass, weedy pavement, brambles, buttress, sky,

A shape less recognisable each week,

A purpose more obscure. I wonder who

40 Will be the last, the very last, to seek

This place for what it was; one of the crew

That tap and jot and know what rood-lofts were?

Some ruin-bibber, randy for antique,

Or Christmas-addict, counting on a whiff

45 Of gown-and-bands and organ-pipes and myrrh?

Or will he be my representative,

Bored, uninformed, knowing the ghostly silt

Dispersed, yet tending to this cross of ground

Through suburb scrub because it held unspilt

50 So long and equably what since is found

Only in separation – marriage, and birth,

And death, and thoughts of these – for which was built

This special shell? For, though I've no idea

55 What this accoutred frowsty barn is worth,

It pleases me to stand in silence here;

A serious house on serious earth it is,

In whose blent air all our compulsions meet,

Are recognized, and robed as destinies.   ⇒

⇒

60 And that much never can be obsolete,

Since someone will forever be surprising

A hunger in himself to be more serious,

And gravitating with it to this ground,

Which, he once heard, was proper to grow wise in,

If only that so many dead lie round.

Philip Larkin

(?) Question

Choose a poem in which the poet/persona experiences a moment of revelation or understanding.

Describe what the moment was about and discuss how the experience or revelation is important to the poem as a whole.

Answer

Below is an outline answer using the six points for 'Answering the questions' on pages 152–53.

1 **Opening paragraph**
   In the poem 'Church Going' by Philip Larkin there is a moment towards the end of the poem when the persona says:
   'It pleases me to stand in silence here;
   A serious house on serious earth it is,'
   He finally comes to a sort of conclusion that religion might just have something to say even to a modern agnostic/atheist such as he is. It is important because in the whole poem up to that point he has been questioning the point of churches and religion in the modern world.

2 **Concluding paragraph**
   The importance of the moment is that it causes us to question our own views on religion. With Larkin we have looked at the parts of the church and its ritual that seem to have no use, but his persona's revelation suggests that there is in people a hunger for spiritual things and that the church might provide at least a place for deep thought.

3 **Reordering/selecting your material**
   In this question an answer really has to start near the end of the poem and then go back to consider the earlier part of the poem.

4 **Central concern(s)**
   The central concern is almost dictated by the question – some sort of hunger for spirituality would be acceptable as a central concern. But there are other possibilities: that such attempts at seeking answers ultimately fail – if you think the last line undercuts everything he has seemed to say. There are many ways of reading any poem and no single, absolutely cast-iron, interpretation.

5 **Quotation/reference**
   The opening paragraph contains a two-line quotation, and in the body of the answer there will be the need to quote, for example, 'some brass and stuff' when discussing the uselessness of some church rituals – 'stuff' being a particularly good example of word choice in this context as it suggests in itself a pile of useless things that nobody can be bothered looking at closely.

⇒

6 **Technical features**

The opening and closing paragraphs illustrated above deal with 'central concerns', and a feature such as word choice has been illustrated in point 5. Features such as these should appear in the course of the essay where they are needed to expand on a point you are making in the course of your argument. But not every quotation needs to be analysed to

death. You may wish to quote in support of a 'psychological' point. For example:
'Yet stop I did: in fact I often do,
And always end much at a loss like this,'
shows how the rather cynical persona of the first two stanzas is perhaps not quite so sure of his views as he thought. This quotation makes a 'character' point and does not need further analysis.

Remember

Don't forget to check your technical accuracy (see page 137).

Example 2 Drama

Macbeth by William Shakespeare

Drama is harder to demonstrate than other genres because if you haven't studied the play chosen for this purpose, it will be less helpful. But it is easy to find a synopsis of a play, and that might help to make the next example more useful.

Macbeth is one of the better known of Shakespeare's tragedies. If you look at a synopsis at www.shakespeare-online.com/plays or the Wikipedia article on *Macbeth* (Plot), you should be able to follow the main points of this answer.

? Question

Choose a play that deals with a conflict such as that between families, generations, couples or social classes.

Describe the conflict and discuss to what extent you find the outcome of the conflict satisfying in terms of the play as a whole.

Answer

1 **Opening paragraph**
In *Macbeth* by William Shakespeare there is a conflict between Macbeth and his wife which ends only with their deaths but, in a sense, their deaths allow Shakespeare in the ending of the play to suggest a better and more settled future for Scotland.

2 **Concluding paragraph**
At the end of the play Macbeth manages to salvage some of his honourable qualities by refusing to surrender to Malcolm, and dying 'with harness on our back' (i.e. in armour, as a soldier). Lady Macbeth's death could be considered less satisfying as she dies by

⇨

suicide, a broken woman, but her death allows Shakespeare to show that although the couple have been in conflict throughout the play, Macbeth still feels great grief when he hears of her death, and it adds to his sense of the inevitable fate, which is sealed in the final scene.

3 **Reordering/selecting your material**

In this case, the order of the material will follow roughly the chronological events of the play, but the selection will be much more important. If you know the play or have read the synopsis, the conflict between Macbeth and Lady Macbeth is followed in only a few, very important, scenes – the letter from Macbeth/the decision or persuasion to Duncan's murder/the murder and its aftermath. The next conflict is over Macbeth's plan to murder Banquo and Fleance – Macbeth does not take her fully into his confidence. The next important scene is the banquet scene, where Lady Macbeth watches Macbeth almost come to pieces and creates a diversion. After that, there is only the reported sleepwalking/the sleepwalking scene and then the news of Lady Macbeth's death just as Macbeth is about to take part in his last battle. Selection is really important. There are large areas of the play that could lead you into irrelevance.

4 **Central concern(s)**

You will have been talking of concerns such as conflict, honour, ambition, cruelty, etc. as you write your answer.

5 **Quotation/reference**

Some really important parts should be illustrated by direct quotation: 'Screw your courage to the sticking-place,/And we'll not fail'; 'To know my deed, 'twere best not know myself'; 'Be innocent of the knowledge, dearest chuck'; something from the banquet scene; 'The thane of Fife, had a wife: where is she now?'; 'She should have died hereafter;/there would have been a time for such a word'; something from Macbeth's speech after her death – 'Tomorrow, and tomorrow, and tomorrow …' and something from the end – see concluding paragraph. You only need six or seven short quotations. Other references will be to events and incidents chosen to show how the conflict in the relationship plays out.

6 **Technical features**

In your answer you will have been dealing with characterisation, conflict, central concerns, possibly dialogue and perhaps climax, all quite naturally. You don't need to drag in other features just to 'analyse'. You have been engaged in analysis and evaluation throughout your answer.

Remember

Don't forget to check your technical accuracy (see page 137).

Author's note: if you want to see what might have happened if Lady Macbeth had remained alive, read David Greig's excellent play *Dunsinane*.

Example 3 Prose fiction

The Great Gatsby *by F. Scott Fitzgerald*

For a novel, the method is similar. This time the example is *The Great Gatsby* by F. Scott Fitzgerald. A brief synopsis can be found on Wikipedia or a longer, more detailed and fairly accurate one on www.cliffnotes.com.

? Question

Choose a novel or short story that has a powerful ending.

Discuss to what extent you feel that the ending is a satisfactory outcome to the novel or short story.

Answer

1 **Opening paragraph**

The Great Gatsby ends with Gatsby's death at the hands of George Wilson, who blames him for the death of his wife, Myrtle. Gatsby is innocent but takes the blame for Daisy, who he has loved and just lost. The fact that he has failed to realise his great dream, which has been to regain Daisy's love by becoming as rich as her husband, Tom, and to take her away from him, leaves Gatsby in limbo, his dream destroyed, his whole future a blank. Thus his sacrifice for her finally gives his death some point.

2 **Concluding paragraph**

This paragraph would deal with your final evaluative comment about the extent to which Gatsby's end was 'satisfactory'; you might include a reference to the fact that almost no one attended his funeral as evidence for your opinion either way.

3 **Reordering/selecting your material**

Here, you have to start with the ending and then decide how far back you want to go to deal with the whole novel. You would probably select material about how he loved and lost Daisy, how the narrator, Nick, lets you see Gatsby through his eyes, and how Nick regarded Gatsby in the end: 'You're worth the whole damn bunch put together.'

4 **Central concern(s)**

One or two of the central concerns – the power of wealth, unattainable dreams, exploitation of little people like Myrtle and George, the carelessness of the rich, etc. – are likely to have been touched on.

5 **Quotation/reference**

Again, as with a play, you should have a small number of key quotations at your fingertips, but mainly you have to refer in detail to important incidents/conversations/settings.

6 **Technical features**

In your answer you will have been dealing with characterisation, the effect of the narrator, central concerns, possibly dialogue and perhaps climax, all quite naturally. You don't need to drag in other features just to 'analyse'. You have been engaged in analysis and evaluation throughout your answer.

Remember

Don't forget to check for technical accuracy (see page 137).

Summary 👍

1 Make sure you read the question carefully before you choose to do it.
2 Get straight to grips with the question in the first paragraph.
3 Select and order your material. You won't be able to use all you know.
4 Your conclusion should arise from the argument of your answer, and will probably contain an overall evaluation of the text and question.
5 Check your technical accuracy.

Non-fiction and film and television drama

Remember the restriction about genres. You cannot answer on non-fiction if you have answered on a Scottish prose text (novel or short story) in Section 1. However, you are perfectly free to choose film and television drama because it does not appear in Section 1.

Questions ❓

Prose: non-fiction

7 Choose a piece of journalism that is concerned with an important contemporary issue – economic, social or political.

Discuss how the writer, by her or his presentation of ideas and evidence, increases your knowledge and understanding of the issue.

8 Choose a book, journal or account which conveys a sense of an exciting, harrowing or dangerous experience.

Discuss how the writer's use of features such as setting, climax and language were important elements in your appreciation of the experience.

9 Choose a work of biography or autobiography that discusses a problem or problems which the subject of the biography or autobiography has had to face.

Briefly describe the problem(s) and discuss to what extent the writer's presentation of the problem(s) creates sympathy for the subject.

Film and television drama

13 Choose a film or television drama that has at its centre a destructive personality.

Discuss how the destructive nature of the character is revealed and how this affects your view of the character in the course of the film or television drama. ⇒

Hints & tips ⭐

Non-fiction

The features of a non-fiction text are more like the features that were discussed in the chapters dealing with the Understanding, Analysis and Evaluation paper.

✓ The writer's stance is particularly important. You should be able to detect from the tone and language which 'view' he/she is promoting.
✓ The evidence – is it convincing?
✓ Is the evidence selective – does it seem to be one-sided?
✓ Is the language emotive – are you persuaded to admire or to condemn?

14 Choose a film or television drama in which a key scene or sequence is intensified by sound and/or visual effects.

Describe how the sound/visual effects intensify the scene or sequence and discuss the importance of the scene to the film or television drama as a whole.

15 Choose a film or television drama that explores a particular stage of life such as childhood or adolescence.

Discuss how the film or programme-makers explore the subject, and discuss to what extent they create a convincing depiction of that stage of life.

The last two examples use question 8 (prose: non fiction) and question 13 (film and television drama) from the sample question bank above to demonstrate the six points on pages 152–53.

Example 4 Prose: non-fiction

Touching the Void *by Joe Simpson*

This book by a mountaineer and philosopher deals with his account of a disastrous expedition to the Peruvian Andes. Wikipedia has a summary and you can find a slightly longer one at sites such as www.bookrags.com.

? Question

Choose a book, journal or account which conveys a sense of an exciting, harrowing or dangerous experience.

Discuss how the writer's use of features such as setting, climax and language were important elements in your appreciation of the experience.

Answer

1 **Opening paragraph**
In *Touching the Void* by Joe Simpson, the writer's ability to recreate his experience is illustrated in his description of the setting on the mountain, his creating of climax – both the moral climax of the book and the physical climax which continues the suspense – and his precise use of word choice and imagery.

2 **Concluding paragraph**
The economical structure of the book – the fact that it starts when they are already on the mountain and finishes with a swift summary of the aftermath of the incident – allows the real focus to fall on the moral dilemma at the heart of the book. What is left seared on the reader's mind is the emotional and realistic description of the painful return, with the associated suspense as to its outcome.

3 **Reordering/selecting your material**
In this case, a chronological approach would

allow discussion of some of the suggested techniques and any other possible techniques you might think of (for example, the technical and detailed mountaineering vocabulary lends verisimilitude).

4 **Central concern(s)**
The central concerns – moral responsibility, supremacy of willpower – will have been part of your argument.

5 **Quotation/reference**
If you choose to deal with description of the setting, word choice or imagery, you would need to have some quotations to illustrate your points.

6 **Technical features**
In the course your answer you will have dealt with structure, climax, setting and possibly language. The question in this case actually demands that you cover a number of features, which you have achieved.

Remember

Don't forget to check your technical accuracy (see page 137).

Example 5 Film and television drama

Francis Ford Coppola's film *The Godfather* is an example of a film which could be used in this question. If you have not seen it, www.imdb.com has a commentary, a very full synopsis and several clips available to view.

(?) Question

Choose a film or television drama that has at its centre a destructive personality.

Discuss how the destructive nature of the character is revealed and how this affects your view of the character in the course of the film or television drama.

Answer

1 **Opening paragraph**

At the beginning of the film the Godfather is portrayed as a destructive character. However, it becomes obvious as the film progresses that it is Michael Corleone who is going to become the truly destructive character, although at the beginning he appears to be striving in the opposite direction.

2 **Concluding paragraph**

These latter scenes, including the sequence of assassinations taking place against the backdrop of a baptism, are especially destructive. This and the subsequent garrotting of Carlo combine to lose Michael any sympathy which his initial predicament might have gained for his character.

3 **Reordering/selecting your material**

The essay would probably revolve round the scenes which reveal the change in Michael – the hospital scene, etc. A lot of the beginning could be omitted. A more in-depth exploration of one of the powerful scenes at the end of the film would illustrate the lengths to which Michael will now go, decreasing the viewer's sympathy.

4 **Central concern(s)**

The central concerns of power and corruption are at the heart of your answer.

5 **Quotation/reference**

As with plays and novels, you should have a stock of short quotations and detailed references you can call on.

6 **Technical features**

You will have been dealing with characterisation throughout, and structural techniques. Filmic techniques will feature in your detailed discussion of a powerful scene. The answer should be based on the changes in Michael's character rather than on a list of particular techniques.

Remember

Don't forget to check your technical accuracy (see page 137).

Acknowledgements

SQA material from *NQ English Writing Folio: Marking Instructions – Higher* from *http:www.sqa.org.uk/files_ccc/WritingFolio-HigherMIS.pdf*, copyright © Scottish Qualifications Authority, reproduced by permission of SQA.

Jon Absalom: 'The truth about life as a househusband' from *The Guardian* (27 October 2005), *http://www.theguardian.com/society/2005/oct/27/childrensservices.familyandrelationships*

Vicky Allan: 'All kids want for Christmas is technology' from the *Sunday Herald*, (15 December 2013), reproduced by permission of Herald & Times Group, www.heraldscotland.com.

Ian Bell: 'Divided we fall' from the *Sunday Herald* (29 December 2013) and 'Is Twitter dumbing us down?' from the *Sunday Herald*, (5 January 2014), reproduced by permission of Herald & Times Group, www.heraldscotland.com.

Libby Brooks: 'So you want them to be happy?' from *The Guardian* (16 September 2006), *http://www.theguardian.com/lifeandstyle/2006/sep/16/familyandrelationships.family*, copyright Guardian News & Media Ltd 2006, reproduced by permission of the publisher.

Joshua Constine: 'You should use Twitter because it makes everyone as smart as anyone' (post on Twitter) from *www.techcrunch.com* (11 November, 2013).

Rachel Cooke: 'To bring girls into sport, get rid of old ideas about 'femininity'' from The Observer (22 February 2014), *http://www.theguardian.com/commentisfree/2014/feb/22/girls-school-sport-femininity*, copyright Guardian News & Media Ltd 2014, reproduced by permission of the publisher.

Carol Ann Duffy: 'Originally' (from *The Other Country*, 1990) from *Selected Poems* (Penguin Books, 1994); 'Mrs Midas' and 'Anne Hathaway' from *The World's Wife* (Picador, 2010).

Terry Eagleton: 'I am not connected' from *Prospect Magazine* (July 2013), reproduced by permission of the publisher.

Barbara Ellen: 'Hunger for success' from *The Observer* (8 June 2014), from *http://www.theguardian.com/commentisfree/2014/jun/08/state-school-pupils-university-lower-entry-requirements*, copyright Guardian News & Media 2014, reproduced by permission of the publisher.

Lawrence Ferlinghetti: from 'The Kiss – Short Story on a Painting of Gustav Klimt', *http://webclass.lakeland.cc.il.us/sphillips/gkthekiss.htm*.

Jonathan Freedland: 'Food banks or dignity: is that the choice we offer the hungry?' from *The Guardian* (21 February 2014), from *http://www.theguardian.com/commentisfree/2014/feb/21/food-banks-dignity-hungry-denial-crisis*, copyright Guardian News & Media 2014, reproduced by permission of the publisher.

Janice Galloway: from *The Trick is to Keep Breathing* (Polygon, 1989), © Janice Galloway 1989.

Suzanne Goldenberg: 'Marine mining: Underwater gold rush sparks fears of ocean catastrophe' from *The Observer* (2 March 2014), *http://www.theguardian.com/environment/2014/mar/02/underwater-gold-rush-marine-mining-fears-ocean-threat*, copyright Guardian News & Media Ltd, 2014, reproduced by permission of the publisher.

Gwen Harwood: 'Surburban Sonnet' from *Selected Poems* (Penguin Australia, 2001).

Robin Jenkins: from *The Cone Gatherers* (1955; Canongate Books, 2004).

India Knight: 'Oh do try to be more feminine, you sporting goddesses' from *The Times* (23 February 2014), *http://www.thesundaytimes.co.uk/sto/comment/columns/indiaknight/article1378595.ece*, reproduced by permission of News Syndication.

Philip Larkin: 'Church Going' from *Philip Larkin: Collected Poems* (Faber and Faber, 1990).

John McGrath: from *The Cheviot, the Stag and the Black Oil* (Methuen Drama, 1981), reproduced by permission of Bloomsbury Publishing plc.

Joanna Moorehead: 'The joys of a 21st century childhood' from *The Independent*, 13 September 2006, *http://www.independent.co.uk/news/uk/this-britain/the-joys-of-a-21stcentury-childhood-415796.html*, reproduced by permission of ESI Media, *www.independent.co.uk*.

Sylvia Patterson: 'Swallow your pride and save our fish' from *The Herald (Glasgow)*, 13 June 2009, *http://www.heraldscotland.com/swallow-your-pride-and-save-our-fish-1.830274* .

Iain Crichton Smith: from *The Painter* and *The Crater* from *The Red Door: The Complete English Short Stories, 1949–76* (Birlinn, 2001).

David Stephen: from *Seven swans* from *String Lug the Fox* (Lutterworth Press, 1950).

Every effort has been made to trace all copyright holders, but if any have been inadvertently overlooked the Publishers will be pleased to make the necessary arrangements at the first opportunity.